lonely planet

POCKET

NICE & MONACO

TOP SIGHTS · LOCAL EXPERIENCES

D0734029

GREGOR CLARK

Contents

Plan Your Trip 4

Vieux Nice (p35)
ARSENIE KRASNEVSKY/SHUTTERSTOCK ©

Welcome to Nice & Monaco

With its mix of real-city grit, belle-époque opulence, year-round sunshine, vibrant street life and a stunning seaside location, no European city compares with Nice. Tiny Monaco, the world's second-smallest country, packs a lot of attitude into its 200 hectares, and is a major draw for hedonists, high-stakes gamblers and Formula One fans.

Place Masséna (p67)

Top Sights

TRABANTOS/SHUTTERSTOCK ©

Promenade des Anglais

The Riviera's legendary beachfront boulevard. **p58**

Cours Saleya Markets

Nice's colourful century-old marketplace. **p36**

Musée Matisse

Hilltop villa with Matisse master-pieces. **p78**

Casino de Monte Carlo

Monaco's iconic belle-époque gambling palace. **p114**

Colline du Château

Nice's window on the Mediterranean. **p38**

LEFT: LKONYA/SHUTTERSTOCK ©; RIGHT: KATATONIA82/SHUTTERSTOCK ©

M. DAGNINO – MUSÉE OCÉANOGRAPHIQUE DE MONACO ©

Musée Océanographique de Monaco

Gateway to Monaco's underwater world. **p118**

Musée d'Art Moderne et d'Art Contemporain (MAMAC) Showcase of avant-garde Niçois artwork. **p94**

ARTAZIUM/SHUTTERSTOCK ©

LEFT: JULIE MAYFENG/SHUTTERSTOCK © @ RIGHT: MAREKUSZ/SHUTTERSTOCK © ©

Musée National Marc Chagall The world's largest Chagall collection. **p80**

Musée Masséna

Treasure trove of belle-époque history. **p62**

Eating

From street food stalls to Michelin-starred restaurants, Nice is a foodie's dream. Traditional Niçois cuisine, influenced by the Mediterranean, the mountains and Italy, still holds centre stage. Yet as befits the French Riviera's culinary capital, a host of contemporary bistros and international restaurants inject variety into the mix.

Mediterranean Roots

Niçois cuisine has its roots in the city's uncommonly mild climate. Olives and wine grapes, which grow easily on the Alpes-Maritimes' sun-drenched hillsides, have been cultivated here since ancient times, along with Mediterranean classics such as tomatoes, peppers, eggplant, zucchini, Swiss chard and aromatic herbs. Adding zest to the mix are locally grown lemons, oranges and other citrus fruits.

International Influences

Neighbouring Italy's impact on Niçois cuisine can be seen in the prevalence of fresh pasta in local shops and restaurants, and in the popularity of Italian desserts. Restaurants around town feature a variety of other international flavours, from Asian to Middle Eastern to North African.

Best Budget Eats

Chez Palmyre Bargain-priced three-course *menus* served in an intimate dining room with wonderful neighbourhood character. (p46)

Acchiardo Long-time local favourite for straight-ahead Niçois cuisine in a convivial stone-walled setting. (p46)

Socca du Cours Niçois street food specialities, served from a humble cart in the Cours Saleya markets. (p44)

La Fougasserie Delicious *pissaladière* (Niçoise pizza) and seasonal treats at Vieux Nice's favourite neighbourhood bakery. (p48)

Kiosque Chez Tintin Beloved hole-in-the-wall near the Libération market, where locals queue for coffee and *pan bagnat* (classic Niçois tuna sandwich). (p88)

IVAN MATEEV/SHUTTERSTOCK ©

Best Bistros & Brasseries

La Femme du Boulanger Choose from open-faced sandwiches or bistro classics, followed by scrumptious desserts. (p71)

Bar des Oiseaux Vintage nightclub decor contrasts with modern cuisine at this perennial Vieux Nice favourite. (p46)

Franchin Classy brasserie backdrop for impeccably prepared Niçois specialities. (p71)

La Rossettisserie Roast meat and veggies in a former bakery remodelled with retro flair. (p46)

Peixes Sit at the counter and watch the chefs at work at Vieux Nice's new seafood superstar. (p45)

Best Veggie & Vegan

Koko Green Raw, vegan and vegetarian fare from around the globe. (p49)

Badaboom Beloved vegan restaurant and juice bar in the trendy port district. (p101)

Best Fine Dining

Flaveur Menus of inventive modern cuisine served in a dining room hung with contemporary art. (p72)

Jan A South African chef works wonders with his creative fusions of flavours. (p101)

Worth a Trip: Fine Dining Meets Sensational Views

Superb cuisine and sensational Mediterranean views converge at **Mirazur** (☏ 04 92 41 86 86; www.mirazur.fr; 30 av Aristide Briand; lunch menus €80-110, dinner menus €110-210; ⏱ 12.15-2pm & 7.15-10pm Wed-Sun Mar-Dec), a 1930s villa with a twinset of Michelin stars overlooking Menton's historic town centre. Take the train to Menton Garavan station (50 minutes from Nice).

Drinking & Nightlife

Whether you're greeting the day with coffee on a Cours Saleya terrace, cooling off at a beach bar along Promenade des Anglais, sipping aperitifs and prowling the backstreet pubs of Vieux Nice, or hopscotching among the wine and cocktail bars of the trend-setting Petit Marais, Nice abounds in atmospheric drinking spots.

Vieux Nice

Vieux Nice is nightlife central, with a nearly unbroken series of bars running parallel to the waterfront along rue St-François de Paule and cours Saleya. Other good bar-hopping streets include rue de la Préfecture, rue Benoît Bunico and rue Rossetti.

Le Petit Marais

A youthful crowd congregates in this bohemian area between place Garibaldi and Port Lympia. Everyone's favourite bar-hopping street is

rue Bonaparte, but the surrounding side streets and the sidewalks facing the port are also packed with revellers.

New Town & Beyond

The waterfront along Promenade des Anglais is lined with beach bars on the Mediterranean side, with cafe terraces and hotel bars across the street. A few blocks inland, the pedestrian zone along rue Masséna is another popular spot for a drink, as is place du Général de Gaulle in Libération.

Best Cafes

Workhouse Café American-style breakfasts and some of Nice's best coffee. (p103)

L'Altra Casa Greet the day at this strategically placed cafe beside Libération's bustling market. (p91)

La Ronronnerie Cats clamber overhead as captivated children share hot chocolate with their parents. (p75)

Best for Beer

Beer District Pick a tap, any tap: 16 draught beers, constantly rotating, and free tastes to boot! (p102)

Brasserie Artisanale de Nice Artisanal beer with an unexpected, traditional Niçois ingredient: chickpeas! (p90)

CARLOS GANDIAGA/SHUTTERSTOCK ©

Ma Nolan's A good old-fashioned, rollicking Irish pub near the Cours Saleya markets. (p51)

Best Drinks with a View

Rooftop 17 Sunset over the city never looked so pretty as from this rooftop bar. (p90)

La Movida Score one point for the cocktails and 10 points for the full-on water-front views. (p50)

La Shounga Hidden away on the back side of Castle Hill, this vibrant bar with a sea-facing terrace is perfect for mojitos overlooking the port. (p51)

Best for Cocktails

El Merkado Cocktails and tapas are the twin draws at this lively Vieux Nice bar. (p50)

Rosalina Bar Aperitifs here come with delicious home-made tapenade. (p102)

Le Café des Chineurs Prime people-watching at the corner of place Garibaldi and rue Bonaparte. (p104)

Best Wine Bars

La Part des Anges Snack and sip wines selected by a true aficionado. (p75)

Café Paulette Chic and sophisticated, with superb wines and tasty tapas. (p100)

Rosé! Dedicated to the proposition that all wines are not created equal; here, pink is the only colour that counts! (p103)

Nice's Best Bar-Hopping Streets

These streets offer fun drinking spots:

○ Rue Bonaparte, Le Port-Garibaldi

○ Rue St-François de Paule and cours Saleya, Vieux Nice

Shopping

Shopping hotspots range from Vieux Nice's vintage boutiques and the New Town's designer fashion temples to the antiques shops and contemporary galleries on the hip streets near place Garibaldi. For quintessentially French gifts, head to Vieux Nice, where you'll find gourmet treats, Provençal soaps, locally made perfume and more.

Epicurean Pleasures

When it comes to food and drink, you're spoiled for choice in Vieux Nice. Wander down virtually any street and you'll find shelves and display windows stocked with enticing products from all over southern France and the Côte d'Azur.

From Boutiques to Antiques

From big-name designer brands to vintage threads with a personal touch, Nice offers fashion

for every taste and budget. High-end shopping is concentrated in the New Town's Carré d'Or neighbourhood, while funkier and more casual boutiques abound in Vieux Nice and the port district. The latter is also home to an abundance of antiques shops.

Best Markets

Cours Saleya Food Market Fruits, veggies, cheeses, olives, baked goods and street snacks from dozens of local producers. (p37)

Cours Saleya Flower Market Roses, mimosas and miniature citrus trees make

this Vieux Nice's sweetest-smelling square. (p37)

Marché de la Condamine This outdoor fruit and veg market offers a rare slice of local life in Monaco. (p137)

Marché de la Libération Vendors spread out over several hundred square metres at this ever-popular morning market. (p91)

Cours Saleya Flea Market Interesting finds abound at this flea market (pictured) that takes over cours Saleya every Monday. (p37)

Best Food Shops

Le Fromage A bounty of local cheeses fills display cases at this Vieux Nice *fromagerie*. (p55)

Pâtisserie LAC Indulge your wildest chocolate dreams

BELLENA/SHUTTERSTOCK ©

at this well-known Niçois shop. (p55)

Maison Auer Worth visiting for its window displays alone, this *confiserie* (confectioner) is a sweet-tooth's dream come true. (p52)

Olio Donato Exceptional hazelnut spread, truffle oil and more from Italy. (p54)

Moulin à Huile d'Olive Alziari Olive oil from the edge of Nice. (p55)

Best Wine Shops

Les Grandes Caves Caprioglio Locals decant bulk wine here, while visitors buy bottles of Bellet. (p54)

Cave de la Tour Wines are available by the bottle or glass at this long-standing neighbourhood shop. (p53)

L'Orangerie Artisanal liqueur from bitter oranges grown in Monaco. (p136)

Best Boutiques

La Boutique du Flacon Antique bottles, perfumes, handbags and accessories fill this tiny boutique. (p54)

Friperie Caprice Travel back in time at Nice's favourite vintage shop. (p53)

Au Bonheur des Cocottes This Petit Marais boutique sells creatively restored vintage finds alongside original artwork. (p105)

Worth a Trip: Atmospheric Market

Among the Côte d'Azur's most colourful shopping experiences is the **Marché Provençal** (cours Masséna; ⏰7am-1pm Tue-Sun Sep-Jun, daily Jul & Aug) in Antibes, 30 minutes by train from Nice. It's a wonderful market selling fruit, vegetables, meat, cheese and local products like tapenade, all atmospherically housed under a cast-iron roof.

Outdoors

Getting outdoors is a way of life in Nice. Swimming and sunbathing by the Med is everyone's favourite summer pastime, along with water sports and walking, cycling or skating along the broad beachfront promenade. Beyond the beach, Nice's inviting parks and squares are the venue for seasonal festivals and everyday recreation.

Parks, Gardens & Squares

Nice is blessed with a multitude of beautiful public spaces, from squares like place Masséna and place Garibaldi to parks commemorating the city's long-obliterated hilltop castle, its Roman ruins and the Paillon River that once flowed through town. Thanks to Nice's abundant sunshine, you'll find people out enjoying these places throughout the year. Down the coast, Monaco's gorgeous gardens are also well worth a visit.

Outdoor Activities

The broad, pedestrian-friendly Promenade des Anglais and quai des États-Unis stretch for several kilometres along Nice's beachfront, offering the city's most delightful and relaxing place for a stroll. Parallel to the pedestrian zone is a recreation path packed with cyclists and skaters revelling in the same full-on Mediterranean views. Various outfits along Nice's waterfront rent out skates, skateboards, bikes, scooters, Segways and water-sports equipment including kayaks and stand-up paddleboards, and organise other activities such as waterski-ing, wakeboarding and paragliding.

Best Spots for a Stroll

Promenade des Anglais Mingle with the summer crowds along Nice's iconic beachfront. (p58)

Promenade du Paillon Join Niçois families out for a walk, or take your own kids out to play on this pedestrian walkway. (pictured; p70)

Jardins St-Martin Enjoy verdant paths, outdoor sculptures and spellbinding clifftop views of Monaco's harbour. (p127)

ROSTISLAV GLINSKY/SHUTTERSTOCK ©

Best Beaches

Plage Publique des Ponchettes Dive into the Med and soak up the sun on Vieux Nice's popular public beach. (p44)

Plage Paloma Aquamarine waters lap this gorgeous crescent of beach between Nice and Monaco. (p111)

Plage Petite Afrique Spectacularly placed below the cliffs in Beaulieu-sur-Mer. (p109)

Best Parks & Gardens

Colline du Château Climb the hill above Vieux Nice to see castle ruins and dazzling views. (p38)

Jardin des Arènes Plan a picnic among the olive trees

and Roman ruins at this park in Cimiez. (p88)

Jardin Exotique Discover the world's most magnificent cactus garden, high on Monaco's steep slopes. (p126)

Roseraie Princesse Grace Over 4000 roses entwine with olive trees in this Monaco public garden. (p128)

Best Outdoor Activities

Glisse Evasion Water-sports specialist on the beach side of Promenade des Anglais. (p70)

Roller Station Choose your preferred rolling method at this agency renting skates, skateboards, scooters and bikes. (p45)

Worth a Trip: Garden with a View

Enjoy spectacular Mediterranean vistas at **Jardin Exotique d'Èze** (☑04 93 41 10 30; www.jardinexotique-eze.fr; rue du Château; adult/child €6/3.50; ☺9am-7.30pm Jul-Sep, to 6.30pm Apr-Jun & Oct, to 4.30pm Nov-Mar), a cactus garden atop the craggy hilltop village of Èze, 30 minutes by bus from Nice.

Museums & Monuments

When you're ready for a break from the beach, Nice and Monaco's cultural attractions offer a welcome alternative. World-class art museums reflect the region's long-standing bohemian appeal, while an assortment of palaces, historic villas, belle-époque hotels and other architectural gems make for fine viewing inside and out.

City of Artists

The Côte d'Azur has ensnared many an artist with the beauty of its light. Not least Henri Matisse, who came here one drizzly winter to convalesce from bronchitis and was so smitten when the sun finally emerged that he made Nice his adoptive home for the next 37 years. Chagall, Picasso and Renoir also fell in love with this place, and the city was later home to the influential avant-garde École de Nice. Art museums abound throughout the region, but Nice's three superstars – the Musées Matisse, Chagall and d'Art Moderne – are reason enough to justify an aesthetic pilgrimage.

Palaces, Villas & Belle-Époque Beauties

Opulence has long been the Côte d'Azur's calling card, as exemplified by Monte Carlo's casino and the hotels along Nice's Promenade des Anglais. Several of the region's palaces and villas have opened their doors as museums, offering visitors a tantalising glimpse of the region's luxurious past.

Collector's Items

From vintage scuba gear to stamps and coins to classic cars, Monaco's museums display some very cool collections. There's no better way to spend a rainy day than visiting them all.

Best Art Museums

Musée Matisse Trace Nice's influence on Matisse's artwork at this museum in a glorious 17th-century villa. (p78)

TARVOS/SHUTTERSTOCK ©

Musée National Marc Chagall Immerse yourself in Chagall's universe at the world's largest museum exclusively devoted to the Belarusian master. (p80)

Musée d'Art Moderne et d'Art Contemporain (MAMAC) Discover the 'new realism' of home-grown Nice artists such as Yves Klein, César and Arman. (p94)

Best for History

Musée Masséna Conjure the magic of belle-époque Nice at this evocative history museum in a late-19th-century villa. (p62)

Palais Princier de Monaco Retrace the footsteps of royalty in the venerable palace of Monaco's princes. (p126)

Best for Architecture

Casino de Monte Carlo No Côte d'Azur creation compares to this unabashedly elegant hilltop casino. (p114)

Hôtel Negresco Nice's most iconic hotel (pictured) is this lavish, domed beauty at the heart of the Promenade des Anglais. (p70)

Best Collections

Musée Océanographique de Monaco Photos, specimens and antique scuba gear invite visitors to dive into the history of undersea exploration. (p118)

Collection de Voitures Anciennes See over a century's worth of snazzy cars from Prince Rainier's personal collection. (p127)

Worth a Trip: An Art-Filled Villa

Villa Ephrussi de Rothschild (☏04 93 01 33 09; www.villa-ephrussi.com/en; adult/child €14/11; ⏱10am-6pm Feb-Jun, Sep & Oct, to 7pm Jul & Aug, 2-6pm Mon-Fri, 10am-6pm Sat & Sun Nov-Jan) is filled with Fragonard paintings, Louis XVI furniture and Sèvres porcelain. Take bus 81 to St-Jean-Cap-Ferrat.

For Kids

Children are well catered for in Nice, with an abundance of beaches, outdoor activities and publicly sponsored kids' events. Nice's tourist office publishes a guide to family travel (http://en.nicetourisme.com/family-friendly-nice), which includes listings of kid-friendly activities, parks, playgrounds and other resources.

Promenade du Paillon

The kilometre-long Promenade du Paillon is Nice's favourite spot for kids to get their wiggles out. Extending from Jardin Albert 1er near the waterfront to Nice's modern art museum, it has a fabulous outdoor playground near its eastern edge (pictured), featuring a variety of whimsical play structures shaped like sea creatures. At the park's western edge near place Masséna, kids love playing in the 128 water jets, which shoot out water and mist at unpredictable intervals and get lit up colourfully at night.

Christmas Village

Christmas in Nice is a festive occasion, with the city's squares and palm trees all lit up and an entire Christmas village set up in Jardin Albert 1er. Families bring their kids out for ice skating, carousels, bouncy castles, rides on the giant Ferris wheel and visits with Père Noël (Santa Claus).

Beaches

Beaches are everywhere in Nice and along the surrounding coastline, and there are plenty of family-friendly accommodation options within a 10-minute walk of the waterfront.

Best for Getting the Wiggles Out

Promenade du Paillon Play in the water jets, run on the grass and climb on the whale and octopus play structures. (pictured; p70)

Parc Princesse Antoinette Join Monaco locals at this playground and minigolf course in a hillside olive grove. (p123)

Best Beaches

Plage Publique des Ponchettes Free public

SOLOMAKHA/SHUTTERSTOCK ©

beach in the heart of Vieux Nice. (p44)

Plage des Fourmis Calm waters and easy access make this Beaulieu-sur-Mer beach a family favourite. (p109)

Best Kids' Activities

Noël à Nice Kids love Nice's Christmas village, filled with fun winter activities. (p22)

Carnaval de Nice Confetti, jugglers, acrobats and parades of giant insects and papier-mâché kings and queens. (p22)

Musée Océanographique de Monaco Gaze at sharks and silly-named tropical fish in Monaco's 6m-tall aquarium tank. (p118)

Palais Princier Watch the changing of the guard outside Monaco's palace. (p126)

Best Food & Drink for Kids

La Ronronnerie Nibble on cake and play (nicely) with the kitties at this cat-themed cafe. (p75)

Gelateria Azzurro Watch the waffle cone-maker in action while awaiting ice-cream treats. (p50)

Chocolaterie de Monaco Enjoy hot cocoa and other chocolatey delights in Monaco's old town. (p132)

Worth a Trip: Petit Parfumeurs

France's perfume capital, Grasse (an hour from Nice by train) invites children aged four to 10 to try their hand at perfume-making at the half-hour Petit Parfumeur workshop offered by **Molinard** (📞 04 92 42 33 21; www.molinard.com; 60 bd Victor Hugo; 20min/1hr/2hr workshops €30/69/189; ⏰ 9.30am-6.30pm).

Festivals & Events

Nice and Monaco's blockbuster events include the Carnaval de Nice in late February, Monaco's Formula One Grand Prix in May and the Nice Jazz Festival in July. A number of smaller events – from sporting competitions to music festivals to seasonal festivities for kids – take place throughout the year.

Carnaval

To experience Nice at its off-season best, visit during the city's exuberant late-February Carnaval. For three weekends and two intervening weeks, Nice's streets fill with colourful parades featuring gigantic papier-mâché figures and displays of locally grown flowers. .

Nice Jazz Festival

France's original jazz festival features a jam-packed six-night calendar of performances on two stages in Jardin Albert 1er,

and fringe concerts popping up all around town, from Vieux Nice to Masséna to the shopping streets around rue de France.

Formula One Grand Prix

Formula One's most iconic event spans four days in late May, when Monaco goes completely car crazy and every street in town is closed for the race. At other times of the year, fans can walk the 3.2km circuit through town; the tourist office has maps. Friday's cheapest tickets go for €30; figure €1400 for a

prime casino-side Sunday spot.

Best Seasonal Celebrations

Carnaval de Nice (www. nicecarnaval.com; ⏱ Feb-Mar) An explosion of colour brightens Nice's wintertime streets, with giant puppet parades and flower-covered floats (pictured).

Noël à Nice (www.nice. fr; ⏱ Dec; c) Ice skating, Ferris wheel rides and visits with Father Christmas make for multigenerational winter fun.

Monaco Art en Ciel (www.monaco-feuxdartifice. mc/en; ⏱ Jul & Aug) This fireworks competition lights up Monaco's skies each summer.

FREDERIC DIDES/SHUTTERSTOCK ©

Best Music Festivals

Nice Jazz Festival (www.nicejazzfestival.fr; ⊙Jul) Nice's verdant central park hosts a stellar live music line-up during this exuberant summer festival.

Les Soirées Estivales (www.departement06.fr; ⊙Jun-Sep) Catch a concert in one of the beautiful Alpes-Maritimes villages just beyond Nice's borders.

Fête du Château (www.feteduchateau.com; Colline du Château; admission free; ⊙late Jun/early Jul) Join this two-evening midsummer party on Nice's favourite hilltop for free music by multiple bands.

Best Sporting Events

Formula One Grand Prix (www.formula1monaco.com; ⊙late May) Race cars zip through Monaco's sinuous streets, from the waterfront to the casino.

Marathon des Alpes-Maritimes (www.marathon06.com; ⊙early Nov) Annual marathon along the seafront between Nice and Cannes.

Best Cultural Festivals

Nuit Européenne des Musées (www.nuitdesmusees.culturecommunication.gouv.fr; ⊙3rd Sat in May) Binge on the arts as museums stay open till midnight.

Lu Festin de Nissa (Jardin des Arènes de Cimiez; ⊙Sun in May) Get a taste of Nice's traditional music, dance and food at this popular spring festival.

Worth a Trip: Oranges & Lemons

In late February, don't miss the quirky **Fête du Citron** (Lemon Festival; www.fete-du-citron.com) in Menton, 40 minutes east of Nice by train, which features gigantic sculptures and floats made from tonnes of citrus fruit.

Entertainment

After the sun sets, Nice's streets keep humming, offering nonstop enticements for night owls. Live music pours from doorways throughout town, especially in Vieux Nice. Other venues, from cinemas to summer music festivals to the city's elegant opera house, keep locals and visitors entertained into the wee hours.

MAURO CARLI/ALAMY STOCK PHOTO ©

Live Music & Dance

Nice's many live music venues include cosy clubs and late-night bars cranking out every musical style from rock to jazz. Both Nice and Monaco also host seasons of opera, dance and classical music at their fabulous old opera houses.

Cinema

Nice's neighbourhood cinemas often show English language movies in *v.o.* (*version originale*, ie undubbed) – as does Monaco's delightful open-air summer movie theatre.

Best Live Music Bars

Shapko A Vieux Nice favourite for its wide-ranging musical mix. (p52)

Wayne's Loud, brash and lively music bar in the heart of Vieux Nice. (p52)

Rascasse Live music and DJs by Monaco's waterfront. (p133)

La Cave Romagnan Locals' bar with Saturday-evening jazz. (p75)

Best Performance Halls

Opéra de Nice Nice's venerable opera house (pictured) features operas, ballets and classical music. (p52)

Opéra de Monte Carlo Neoclassical beauty next to Monaco's casino. (p135)

Best Cinemas

Monaco Open-Air Cinema Summertime movies under the stars at Monaco's 3D open-air cinema. (p135)

Cinéma Mercury Favourite cinema on place Garibaldi, Nice's nightlife hub. (p105)

Cinéma Rialto Watch original undubbed films near Nice's beachfront. (p75)

Tours & Courses

A variety of tours, courses and excursions offer the opportunity to delve deeper into the scenery and culture of Nice and the surrounding Alpes-Maritimes département. Explore Nice's gorgeous coastline by boat, take a walking tour of Vieux Nice, go wine-tasting or join a cooking class.

KIEV.VICTOR/SHUTTERSTOCK ©

Centre du Patrimoine

(📞04 92 00 41 90; www.nice.fr/fr/culture/patrimoine; 14 rue Jules Gilly; tours adult/child €5/free; ⏰9am-1pm & 2-5pm Mon-Thu, to 3.45pm Fri) Every weekday, this highly recommended municipal agency offers inexpensive two-hour walking tours of the city with professional local guides. For English-language tours, book two days in advance. The tourist office and website have a full listing of current walks.

The French Way

(📞06 27 35 13 75; www.thefrenchway.fr) Bilingual guide Marion Pansiot leads wonderful cooking classes and themed walking tours focusing on Niçois food and drink, perfume and other topics of cultural interest.

Les Petits Farcis

(www.petitsfarcis.com; 12 rue St-Joseph; course per person incl lunch €195; ⏰9.30am-3pm, dates by arrangement) For over a decade, veteran food writer and cookbook author Rosa Jackson has been teaching cooking classes in her Vieux Nice studio. The morning begins with a shopping trip to the Cours Saleya food market and ends with a leisurely lunch of Niçois delicacies. Classes are tailored to participants' interests and dietary restrictions.

Trans Côte d'Azur

(www.trans-cote-azur.com; quai Lunel; ⏰Apr-Oct; 🚌2 to Port Lympia) Down at Nice's port, this agency runs one-hour boat cruises along the Baie des Anges and Rade de Villefranche from April to October. From late May to September it also sails to Île Ste-Marguerite (one hour), St-Tropez (2½ hours), Monaco (45 minutes) and Cannes (one hour).

Château de Bellet

(📞04 93 37 81 57; www.chateaudebellet.com; 482 chemin de Saquier; ⏰10.30am-6.30pm May-Sep, 10am-noon & 2-5.30pm Tue-Sat Oct-Apr; 🚌62 to Chemin Saquier) The hills above Nice are home to Bellet, one of France's smallest wine *appellations*. Dating to 1941, Bellet is highly sought after – there are just a dozen or so producers, including this wonderful estate 9km northwest of Nice. Call ahead to arrange a vineyard and cellar tour, culminating with tastings.

Four Perfect Days

Day 1

ROSTISLAV GLINSKY/SHUTTERSTOCK ©

Day 2

DROZDIN VLADIMIR/SHUTTERSTOCK ©

Spend the morning exploring Vieux Nice's labyrinth of backstreets. After a leisurely wander through the **Cours Saleya produce and flower markets** (pictured; p37), discover the Baroque beauty of **Cathédrale Ste-Réparate** (p45) and browse charming shops such as **La Boutique du Flacon** (p54).

In the afternoon, after a vegan lunch at **Koko Green** (p49) or a three-course bistro *menu* at **Bar des Oiseaux** (p46), climb **Colline du Château** (p38) for gorgeous views of the old town. Afterwards, sunbathe till sundown on **Plage Publique des Ponchettes** (p44).

Kick off the evening with aperitifs at **La Movida** (p50) and dinner at **Olive et Artichaut** (p48), then finish it off with live music at **Shapko** (p52) or **Wayne's** (p52).

Depending on the weather and your mood, head outdoors to beautiful **Promenade du Paillon** (p70) and **place Masséna** (p67), go designer shopping in the **Carré d'Or** (p67), or discover Nice's high society history at **Musée Masséna** (p62).

Break for a brasserie lunch at **Franchin** (p71), then spend the afternoon along Nice's fabled **Promenade des Anglais** (p58), sipping drinks at **Sporting Plage** (p73), or lounging in one of Nice's trademark blue chairs (pictured).

After dining bistro-style on the sidewalk at **La Femme du Boulanger** (p71) or feasting on gourmet fare at **Flaveur** (p72), cap off the evening with drinks at **Hôtel Negresco** (p70)'s belle-époque bar and a pre-bedtime stroll along the palm-lined beachfront.

Day 3

KIEV.VICTOR/SHUTTERSTOCK ©

Start your day in Libération district, sipping coffee at **L'Altra Casa** (p91), browsing small producers' stalls at **Marché de la Libération** (p91) and tasting beer at **Brasserie Artisanale de Nice** (p90).

Grab a classic *pan bagnat* (Niçois tuna sandwich) at **Kiosque Chez Tintin** (p88), then enjoy an art-focused afternoon in Cimiez. Tour the magnificent **Musée Matisse** (p78), housed in a hilltop villa, and stroll through olive groves and **Roman ruins** (pictured; p88) to the artist's **grave** (p87). Afterwards, explore Marc Chagall's fantastical world at the **Musée Chagall** (p80).

In the evening, sample ceviche at **Peixes** (p45) before a concert at **Opéra de Nice** (p52) or a tour of Vieux Nice's terrace bars.

Day 4

M.LBOYERJ/SHUTTERSTOCK ©

Begin with coffee at **Workhouse Café** (p103) or brunch at **Déli Bo** (p101). Next, delve into the avant-garde art of Nice-based artists like Yves Klein and Niki de Saint Phalle at the **Musée d'Art Moderne et d'Art Contemporain** (p94), and soak up skyline views from the museum's rooftop terrace.

After lunching on *socca* (chickpea-flour pancakes) and other traditional Niçois snacks at **Chez Pipo** (p101), embark from Nice's port for a **cruise** (p100) along the villa-dotted coastline near Villefranche-sur-Mer (pictured; p107).

In the evening, dine on gourmet fare at **Jan** (p101) or tapas and wine at **Café Paulette** (p100), then bar-hop through the Petit Marais, lingering at hotspots like **Rosé!** (p103) and **Beer District** (p102).

Need to Know

For detailed information, see Survival Guide p139

Currency
Euro (€)

Language
French

Visas
Not required for citizens of most countries for stays up to 90 days. Passports should be valid for at least three months beyond return date from France. Generally no restrictions for EU citizens.

Money
ATMs widely available. Credit cards accepted in most hotels and restaurants.

Mobile Phones
GSM and 4G networks available through inexpensive SIM cards.

Time
Central European Time (GMT/UTC plus one hour)

Tipping
Not required in restaurants (bills automatically include a 15% service charge).

Daily Budget

Budget: Less than €130
Dorm bed: €25–50
Double room in a budget hotel: €80
Street food or lunch *menu* (set meal): less than €25
One-week public transport ticket: €15

Midrange: €130–220
Double room in a midrange hotel: €90–190
Dinner *menu* in midrange restaurant: €30–50
One-week ticket to Nice's municipal museums: €20

Top end: More than €220
Double room in a top-end hotel: €190–350
Lunch or dinner in gastronomic restaurant: €65–100
Prime seats at Opéra de Nice: €82

Advance Planning

Three months before Book tickets for major events such as Monaco Grand Prix and the Nice Jazz Festival. Book accommodation if visiting in peak summer season (July and August).

One month before Book tickets for seats in the stands at Carnaval de Nice.

One week before Make reservations at restaurants, especially in peak summer season.

Arriving in Nice

Most travellers will arrive in Nice by air or rail.

✈ Nice Côte d'Azur Airport

Bus 98 runs to Vieux Nice (€6, 30 minutes), bus 99 to Nice Ville train station (€6, 30 minutes) and tram 2 (scheduled for completion in 2019) to place Garibaldi and the port (20 to 25 minutes).

🚆 Nice Ville Train Station

Tram 1 (€1.50) runs north to Libération (five minutes) or southeast to Vieux Nice (10 minutes) and place Garibaldi (15 minutes).

⚓ Port de Nice

Tram 2 (€1.50) runs to place Garibaldi (five minutes) and points west throughout the New Town.

Getting Around

Nice's excellent public transport system, operated by Lignes d'Azur (📞 08 10 06 10 06; www.lignesdazur. com), includes a modern, dependable fleet of trams and buses, with the brand-new tram line 2 radically improving access to the port and airport in 2019.

🚋 Tram

The tram is generally your best bet for journeys between the train station, the airport, the port and the city centre.

🚌 Bus

Buses are more useful for destinations along the beachfront and in outlying areas like Cimiez.

🚲 Bicycle

The city's bike-share program Vélo Bleu (📞 04 93 72 06 06; www. velobleu.org) offers a low-cost way to explore Nice.

Nice & Monaco Neighbourhoods

Le Port-Garibaldi (p93)
Brimming with bohemian bistros, bars and boutiques, Le Port-Garibaldi is Nice's nightlife hub, and the bustling launch point for coastal boat excursions and ferries to Corsica.

Cimiez, Libération & Vernier (p77)
Hillside Cimiez is home to mansions, art museums and Roman ruins; the residential neighbourhoods just below offer an engaging slice of everyday Niçois life.

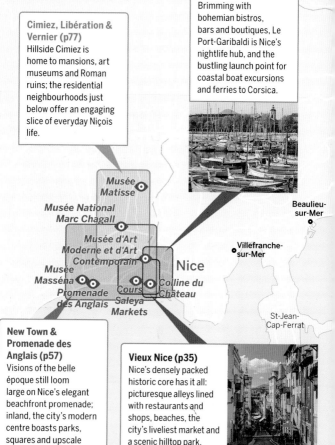

Musée Matisse

Musée National Marc Chagall

Musée d'Art Moderne et d'Art Contemporain

Musée Masséna

Promenade des Anglais

Cours Saleya Markets

Nice

Colline du Château

Beaulieu-sur-Mer

Villefranche-sur-Mer

St-Jean-Cap-Ferrat

New Town & Promenade des Anglais (p57)
Visions of the belle époque still loom large on Nice's elegant beachfront promenade; inland, the city's modern centre boasts parks, squares and upscale shopping.

Vieux Nice (p35)
Nice's densely packed historic core has it all: picturesque alleys lined with restaurants and shops, beaches, the city's liveliest market and a scenic hilltop park.

La Turbie

Monaco

Casino de
Monte Carlo

Musée
Océanographique
de Monaco

Èze

Èze-
sur-Mer

Monaco (p113)
Synonymous with its glitzy
casino, princely palace
and Formula 1 Grand
Prix, Monaco also offers
a wealth of museums,
gardens, villas and
fabulous Mediterranean
views.

Explore
Nice & Monaco

Vieux Nice (p35) ROSTISLAV GLINSKY/SHUTTERSTOCK ©

Vieux Nice

Tucked into a tidy pedestrian-friendly triangle between a leafy green promontory and the sparkling blue Med, Nice's oldest neighbourhood is an aesthetic delight. Vieux Nice's narrow streets, overhung with photogenic ochre-toned 18th-century houses, boast enough markets, bars, bistros and boutiques to build an entire vacation around. Best of all, the beach is never more than five minutes away.

To catch Vieux Nice at its early-morning best, climb Colline du Château (p38) to hear the cathedral bells and watch sun streaming over the domes and rooftops. Grab a snack at La Fougasserie (p48) and wander through the Cours Saleya markets (p36), or join a Vieux Nice walking tour with The French Way (p25) or Centre du Patrimoine (p25). After lunch at local favourite Chez Palmyre (p46), shop for vintage finds at Friperie Caprice (p53), sample sweets at Maison Auer (p52) or sunbathe on Plage des Ponchettes (p44). In the evening, people-watch over apéritifs at Les Distilleries Idéales (p51) before dinner at La Rossettisserie (p46), followed by live music at Shapko (p52).

Getting There & Around

Vieux Nice is compact and pedestrian-friendly. Once you've arrived, it's easiest and most enjoyable to explore the neighbourhood on foot.

🚋 Line 1 to Opéra-Vieille Ville or Cathédrale-Vieille Ville.

🚌 Line 98 from Nice Côte d'Azur Airport.

Neighbourhood Map on p42

Top Sight 📷
Cours Saleya Markets

No place is more emblematic of Nice's old town that this colourful pedestrianised market square, stretching 250m east–west along the city's old ramparts, one block in from the Mediterranean below the city's historic castle hill. In 1861 Nice's original market for fruit, vegetables and flowers was established here, and a more than a century and a half later it's still going strong.

◉ MAP P42, D4

cours Saleya

🕑 6am-5.30pm Tue-Sat, 6.30am-1.30pm Sun

Flower Market

On market days, a sea of colours and fragrances fills cours Saleya's western end (pictured): roses, lilies, mimosas, carnations, jasmine, orange blossoms, violets and more. Flowering plants thrive in Nice's uniquely mild microclimate, thanks to the Alps' dizzying plunge into the Mediterranean here, which creates a protective wall shielding the coast from frigid northern weather. Flowers have been the mainstay of the local perfume economy since the 18th century. Unlike the produce market, which winds down around lunchtime, vendors here stick around all afternoon, selling everything from roses to miniature lemon and kumquat trees to lavender sachets and a rainbow of Provençal soaps.

Food Market

Two city blocks' worth of stalls line the Cours Saleya **produce market** (🕑6am-1.30pm Tue-Sun), laden with seasonal Mediterranean produce from small farmers: multihued organic tomatoes, tiny purple artichokes, long green pods of broad beans, delicately fluted zucchini blossoms, teensy Niçoise olives and piles of freshly harvested citrus from neighbouring Menton. On weekends, cheesemakers descend from the Alpine foothills with locally produced sheep- and goat's-milk cheeses and burrata from across the Italian border.

Flea Market

On Mondays, cours Saleya's produce and flower markets take the day off, making way for a lively all-day *brocante* (Marché à la Brocante; flea market; 🕑7am-6pm Mon). Stalls here display everything from antique furniture to vintage jewellery, coins, stamps, silver, porcelain, crystal and kitchenware. With more than 100 vendors, it's worth lingering a while. Don't hesitate to bargain, as posted prices typically run high.

★ Top Tips

○ Saturday and Sunday are the best days to catch sheep- and goat's-milk cheeses, brought down by farmers from the high pastures of the Alpes-Maritimes.

○ The flower and produce markets are both closed on Mondays – though the flea market makes an engaging alternative.

○ On balmy spring and summer evenings (mid-May to mid-September), a local artisans' market takes over cours Saleya from 6pm till midnight.

○ Artist Henri Matisse surveyed this scene every morning from his studio window on place Charles Félix (it's the golden-hued building at the market's eastern end).

✕ Take a Break

At lunchtime, duck into family-run Ac-chiardo (p46) for fabulous traditional Niçois fare.

People-watch from the sidewalk over coffee, beer or wine at Les Distilleries Idéales (p51).

Top Sight 📷
Colline du Château

For the best views over Nice's red-tiled rooftops, climb the staircases up to Colline du Château, the wooded outcrop on the eastern edge of the old town. This verdant hilltop was chosen as a military outpost by Greek sailors in the 4th century BC. For two millennia it remained fortified, and its modern-day name – meaning Castle Hill – bears witness to the impressive medieval château that once crowned the summit.

◎ MAP P42, G5

Castle Hill

admission free

🕑 8.30am-8pm Apr-Sep, to 6pm Oct-Mar

(Nearly) Impregnable Fortress

Over the centuries, countless invaders tried in vain to conquer Nice's fortified hilltop. During the Franco-Turkish siege in 1543, troops under the command of Barbarossa were on the verge of taking the château when – as legend would have it – a Turkish soldier raising his flag in victory incurred the wrath of the humble washerwoman Caterina Segurana, who proceeded to whack him over the head with her washing paddle.

Caterina's gesture offered encouragement to the Niçois, allowing them to hold out until Charles III, Duke of Savoy, arrived to send the Franco-Turkish forces packing. It remains a defining moment for Nice's civic identity, and Caterina Segurana remains one of the city's heroic figures, commemorated in various statues about town.

The castle finally met its match in 1706, when the French king Louis XIV succeeded in smashing it to smithereens. (Incidentally, he wasn't trying to subdue his own people; Nice was still part of the rival kingdom of Savoy at the time!)

View from the Top

From Vieux Nice, staircases wind up to the hilltop (now a city park), or you can take the free **lift** (Ascenseur du Château; rue des Ponchettes; ⏱9am-8pm Jun-Aug, to 7pm Apr, May & Sep, 10am-6pm Oct-Mar). Up top, after admiring panoramic vistas of the Promenade des Anglais from the **Tour Bellanda**, stroll over to the **Cascade du Casteu** (an artificial 18th-century waterfall, pictured), or wander among the cypresses and ornate tombstones of the 18th-century **Cimitière du Château**. Throughout the park there are exceptional views stretching west–east from Vieux Nice to the port, and north–south from the Alps to the Mediterranean. It's a delightfully shady picnic spot on a hot summer's day.

★ Top Tips

○ Don't freak out when the cannon goes off at noon. It's been faithfully announcing lunchtime on this same hilltop for over 150 years.

○ Yes, there *is* gain without pain! Take the free elevator up the hill from the waterfront and enjoy the views without breaking a sweat.

○ Despite the park's name, don't expect to find a castle up here. The eponymous château was destroyed in 1706 by Louis XIV (back before Nice became part of France).

✗ Take a Break

Stop in for ice cream, coffee or a sandwich at the hilltop **La Citadelle** snack bar.

Descend back to sea level for drinks and waterfront views at La Movida (p50).

Walking Tour 🥾

Vieux Nice Historical Circuit

Traces of Nice's multilayered history are everywhere in Vieux Nice. Starting at Colline du Château – where Greek sailors established the fortified settlement of Nikaïa in 350 BC – this walking circuit takes you through the neighbourhood's medieval streets, past the Baroque cathedral and 19th-century opera house, through the market and along the beachfront, before climbing back up Castle Hill for panoramic views.

Walk Facts

Start Place St-Augustin
End Colline du Château
Length 2km; one hour

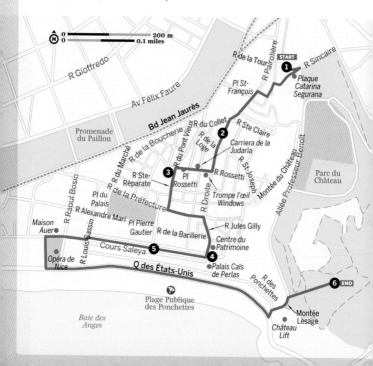

❶ Birthplace of the City

Begin your exploration in place St-Augustin, at the foot of **Colline du Château (Castle Hill)**, whose strategic vantage point overlooking the Mediterranean made it Nice's defensive stronghold from Greek times through the early 1700s. Before you is a plaque honouring Caterina Segurana, the city's washerwoman heroine, who famously rebuffed a Franco-Turkish siege and saved the hill from capture in 1543.

❷ Medieval Streets

Head south on **rue Droite**, the 13th-century thoroughfare for Nice's lucrative salt trade. Turn right on rue Rossetti, noticing the sneaky trompe l'œil windows to your left. Some shutters here are real, others are fake – can you tell which? One block west, notice the sign for Carriera de la Judarìa, the heart of Nice's medieval Jewish quarter.

❸ Baroque Centrepiece

Cathédrale Ste-Réparate (p45) soon comes into view. Today this 17th-century Baroque beauty is the centrepiece of Vieux Nice. It's named for Nice's patron, Ste Réparate, a 3rd-century Palestinian Christian martyr whose body was legendarily transported across the Mediterranean by angels. Place Rossetti, the square before the church, shows strong Italian stylistic influences in its tall shutters and red-and-yellow colour scheme.

❹ Matisse's Studio

Zigzag south to the eastern end of cours Saleya. At 14 rue Gilles Jilly, the Centre du Patrimoine leads wonderful tours of Vieux Nice; to its right at 1 place Charles Félix is the grand golden-hued **Palais Caïs de Pierlas**, where Matisse had his studio from 1921 to 1938.

❺ Cours Saleya to the Opéra

Walk west down cours Saleya, enjoying the colours, sights and smells of Nice's favourite **produce and flower markets** (p36). Further down on the right, glance in at Maison Auer (p52), a fifth-generation confectioner's shop famous for its chocolates and candied fruits. On the left is Nice's venerable late-19th-century opera house (p52).

❻ From the Beach to Castle Hill

Turn left towards the Mediterranean and follow quai des États-Unis east to Nice's popular public beach, Plage Publique des Ponchettes (p44). Across the street, hop aboard the lift (p39) for a free ride to hilltop **Colline du Château** (p38), where you can enjoy bird's-eye views of every place on the route you just walked.

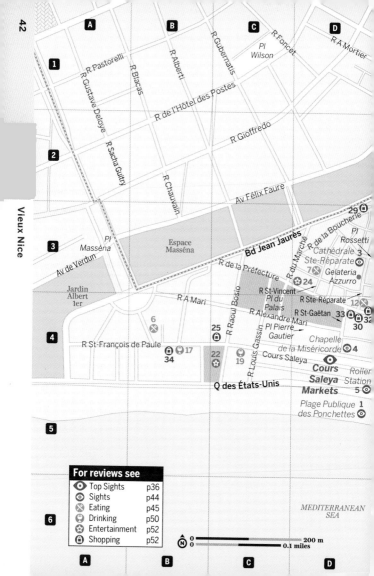

Vieux Nice

	A	B	C	D

1 R Pastorelli
R Gustave Deloye
R Blacas
R Alberti
R Gubernatis
R Foncet
Pl Wilson
R A Mortier

R de l'Hôtel des Postes

2 R Sacha Guitry
R Chauvain
R Gioffredo

Av Félix Faure

3 Pl Masséna
Av de Verdun
Espace Masséna
Bd Jean Jaurès
R de la Préfecture
R du Marché
R de la Boucherie
Pl Rossetti
Cathédrale **3** Ste-Réparate ◉
7 ◉ **24** Gelateria Azzurro

4 Jardin Albert 1er
R A Mari
R Raoul Bosio
R St-Vincent
Pl du Palais
R Alexandre Mari
Pl Pierre Gautier
R Ste-Réparate
R St-Gaëtan **33** ◉ **32**
30
Chapelle de la Miséricorde ◉ **4**
6 ✕
R St-François de Paule
34 ◉ ◉ **17**
25 ◉
22 ✪
19 ◉
R Louis Gassin
Cours Saleya
Cours Saleya Markets ◉
Roller Station **5** ◉
Q des États-Unis
Plage Publique **1** des Ponchettes ◉

5

6

MEDITERRANEAN SEA

For reviews see
◉	Top Sights	p36
◉	Sights	p44
✕	Eating	p45
◯	Drinking	p50
✪	Entertainment	p52
◉	Shopping	p52

Ⓝ 0 ——————— 200 m
0 ——————— 0.1 miles

	A	B	C	D

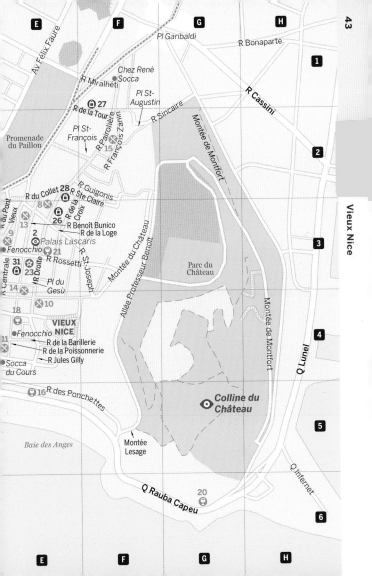

Av Félix Faure

Pl Garibaldi

R Bonaparte

R Miralhéti

Chez René
Socca

Pl St-
Augustin

R Cassini

27

R de la Tour

Pl St-
François

R Sincaire

Montée de Montfort

Promenade
du Paillon

R Parolière

R François Zanin

15

R Guigonis

R du Collet 28 R Ste Claire

8

R de la Croix

26 13

R Benoît Bunico

R de la Loge

Palais Lascaris

2

Montée du Château

Allée Professeur Benoît

Parc du
Château

9

Fenocchio 21

R Rossetti

R St-Joseph

31 23

14

Pl du
Gesù

10

Montée de Montfort

18

VIEUX
NICE

Fenocchio

11

R de la Barillerie
R de la Poissonnerie
R Jules Gilly

Socca
du Cours

16 R des Ponchettes

Baie des Anges

Montée
Lesage

Colline du
Château

Q Tunnel

Q Internet

Q Rauba Capeu

20

Nice's Favourite Savoury Snack

Looking for a quintessentially local eating experience? Don't miss Nice's favourite street snack: *socca*, a savoury, griddle-fried pancake made from chickpea flour and olive oil. Pressed into large metal pans and baked pizza-style in wood-burning ovens, it emerges piping hot and gets instantly chopped into individual servings, known as *parts*. At the best places, there's always a line of people waiting for their *part*, which typically comes served on a humble paper plate, sprinkled with a liberal dose of black pepper. There's no more distinctively Niçois flavour, and while many visitors don't know what to make of it at first, its appeal tends to grow over time. A couple of the old town's favourite haunts:

Socca du Cours (Map p42, E4; place Charles Félix; socca €3, other snacks from €2; ⏰9.30am-1pm) In the heart of the Cours Selaya markets, this no-frills stand draws crowds every morning for its hot-from-the-oven *socca* – delivered every few minutes by bicycle – along with assorted Niçois snacks: stuffed cabbage, *tourte de blette* (chard tart with raisins, pine nuts and parmesan), octopus salad and *pissaladière* – onion tart made the old-fashioned way with *pissala* (anchovy paste, from Niçard dialect for 'salted fish').

Chez René Socca (Map p42, F1; ☎04 93 92 05 73; 2 rue Miralhéti; small plates €3-6; ⏰9am-9pm Tue-Sun, to 10.30pm Jul & Aug, closed Nov; 🌱) Don't expect service with a smile at this chaotic, no-frills corner restaurant – but do expect a stellar slice of *socca*, served alongside plates of *beignets de sardines* (sardine fritters) or *petits farcis* (stuffed vegetables), just like *grande-mère* used to make. Streetside seating is available if you buy a drink (wine, beer, coffee etc) from the bar across the street.

Sights

Plage Publique des Ponchettes

BEACH

1 ◎ MAP P42, D5

Right opposite Vieux Nice, this is generally the busiest beach of all, with oiled bodies either baking in the sun or punching a ball on the beach-volleyball court.

Palais Lascaris

HISTORIC BUILDING

2 ◎ MAP P42, E3

Baroque Palais Lascaris is a 17th-century mansion housing a frescoed orgy of Flemish tapestries, faience and gloomy religious paintings, along with a collection of period musical instruments. On the ground floor is an 18th-century pharmacy. (☎04 93 62 72 40; 15 rue Droite; museum pass 24hr/7 days

€10/20, guided visit adult/child €6/free; ⏱10am-6pm Wed-Mon late Jun–mid-Oct, from 11am mid-Oct–late Jun)

Cathédrale Ste-Réparate CATHEDRAL

3 ◉ MAP P42, D3

One of Nice's Baroque architectural gems, honouring the city's patron saint. (📞04 93 92 01 35; place Rossetti; ⏱2-6pm Mon, 9am-noon & 2-6pm Tue-Sun)

Chapelle de la Miséricorde CHURCH

4 ◉ MAP P42, D4

This 1740 chapel is renowned for its exceptionally rich architecture. (📞04 92 00 41 90; cours Saleya; ⏱2.30-5pm Tue Sep-Jun)

Roller Station SKATING

5 ◉ MAP P42, D5

For a fantastic family outing, rent inline skates, skateboards, scooters and bicycles here to whizz along Nice's Promenade des Anglais. You'll need some ID as a deposit. Count an extra €1/2 per hour/day for protective gear (helmet and pads). (📞04 93 62 99 05; www.roller-station.fr; 49 quai des États-Unis; skates, boards & scooters per hour/day €5/12, bicycles €5/15; ⏱9am-8pm Jul & Aug, 10am-7pm May, Jun, Sep & Oct, to 6pm Nov-Apr)

Eating

Peixes SEAFOOD €€

6 ✖ MAP P42, B4

This chic modern seafood eatery is the latest jewel in the crown of

Cathédrale Ste-Réparate

Niçois master restaurateur Armand Crespo. All done up in white-and-turquoise nautical decor, with dangling fish eyeball light fixtures and murals of a tentacle-haired mermaid ensnaring a fishing boat, it specialises in fresh local fish turned into delicious ceviches, tartares and Japanese-style tatakis by chefs in the open kitchen. (📞04 93 85 96 15; 4 rue de l'Opéra; small plates €12-19, mains €17-35; ⏲noon-10pm Tue-Sat)

Bar des Oiseaux   FRENCH €€

7 🍴 MAP P42, D3

Hidden down a narrow backstreet, this old-town classic has been in business since 1961, serving as a popular nightclub before reincarnating itself as a restaurant (some of its original saucy murals have survived the transition). Nowadays it's a lively bistro serving superb traditional French cuisine spiced up with modern twists. The weekday lunch special offers phenomenal value. Book ahead. (📞04 93 80 27 33; 5 rue St-Vincent; 3-course lunch menu €20, dinner menus from €30; ⏲noon-1.45pm & 7.15-9.45pm Tue-Sat)

Chez Palmyre   FRENCH €

8 🍴 MAP P42, E3

Look no further for authentic Niçois cooking than this packed, cramped, convivial little space in the heart of the old town. The menu is very meat-heavy, with plenty of tripe, veal, pot-cooked chicken and the like, true to the traditional tastes of Provençal cuisine. It's a bargain, and understandably popular. Book well ahead, even for lunch. (📞04 93 85 72 32; 5 rue Droite; 3-course menu €18; ⏲noon-1.30pm & 7-9.30pm Mon, Tue, Thu & Fri)

La Rossettisserie   FRENCH €

9 🍴 MAP P42, E3

Roast meat is the order of the day here: make your choice from beef, chicken, veal or lamb, and pair it with a choice of mashed or sautéed potatoes, ratatouille or salad. Simple and sumptuous, with cosy, rustic decor and a delightful vaulted cellar. (📞04 93 76 18 80; www.larossettisserie.com; 8 rue Mascoïnat; mains €16.50-19.50; ⏲noon-2pm & 7-10pm Mon-Sat)

Acchiardo   FRENCH €

10 🍴 MAP P42, E4

Warm service and irreproachable quality are the hallmarks of this traditional neighbourhood restaurant, which has been run by the same family since 1927. Locals and holidaymakers pack into the three stone-walled rooms for Niçois delights such as *merda di can* (little green gnocchi – nicknamed 'dog poop' for the shape, not the flavour, mind you!), red mullet with parsleyed green beans and olive tapenade, and tiramisu. (📞04 93 85 51 16; 38 rue Droite; mains €16-19; ⏲noon-2pm & 7-10pm Mon-Fri)

The Niçois
Culinary Lexicon

Nice's colourful cuisine is a highlight of any trip. Don't miss these regional specialties:

Aïoli On Fridays, look for this local classic featuring codfish, boiled vegetables and delicious garlicky mayonnaise.

Barbajuans Deep-fried pasta pockets stuffed with Swiss chard, onions, parsley, rice and grated cheese.

Beignets de fleurs de courgettes Zucchini blossom fritters.

Bugnes These dreamy, doughy fritters perfumed with orange blossoms appear in Nice's bakeries around Carnaval time.

Capoun Stuffed cabbage roll, typically filled with meat, rice, eggs, cheese, onions and/or parsley.

Daube provençale Hearty beef stew with red wine and veggies.

Merda di can Lest you wonder, the name – which translates politely as 'dog poop' – refers to the cylindrical shape of these chard-and-potato green gnocchi.

Pan bagnat Classic Niçois sandwich of tuna and/or anchovies served with hard-boiled egg, olives, tomatoes, peppers and other raw veggies on a roll drizzled with olive oil.

Petits farcis Mixed vegetables (tomatoes, peppers, aubergines and/or zucchini) stuffed with ground meat, garlic, parsley and breadcrumbs.

Pissaladière A scrumptious tart of caramelised onions spread over a bed of anchovy paste and topped with black Niçoise olives.

Salade niçoise Most Niçois chefs agree that a proper *salade niçoise* should include tomatoes, green onions, hard-boiled eggs, anchovies, olives, peppers and/or tuna – perhaps supplemented by raw purple artichokes, radishes, celery and/or broad beans – but they generally eschew the boiled potatoes and green beans favoured in many foreign versions!

Socca A savoury chickpea pancake.

Tourte aux blettes A pie made with Swiss chard, raisins, pine nuts, apples, egg and cheese, sometimes sprinkled with powdered sugar.

Cornerstones of a Bistro Empire

Several of Nice's best eateries are owned by pioneering restaurateur Armand Crespo. Peixes (p45) and Bar des Oiseaux (p46) are the latest additions to Crespo's empire, but his original two bistros also merit a visit.

Le Bistrot d'Antoine (04 93 85 29 57; 27 rue de la Préfecture; mains €15-28; noon-2pm & 7-10pm Tue-Sat) A quintessential French bistro, right down to the checked tablecloths, streetside tables and impeccable service – not to mention the handwritten blackboard, loaded with classic dishes such as rabbit pâté, pot-cooked pork, blood sausage and duck breast. If you've never eaten classic French food, this is definitely the place to start; and if you have, you're in for a treat.

Le Comptoir du Marché (04 93 13 45 01; 8 rue du Marché; mains €15-18; noon-2pm & 7-9.30pm Tue-Sat) With its vintage kitchen decor and great-value prices, the Comptoir does predictably well. There are five or six daily mains, scribbled on a chalkboard. The cuisine is a modern twist on traditional French recipes, with lots of offal and staples such as *magret de canard* (duck breast), confit rabbit and *joue de cochon* (pork cheek).

La Fougasserie

BAKERY €

11 MAP P42, E4

Vieux Nice's finest baked goods emanate from this little corner *boulangerie,* which also operates a stall in the Cours Saleya food market. Quality organic ingredients go into a full spectrum of sweet and savoury delights, including croissants, *pan bagnat* (Niçois tuna sandwich), pizza and *pissaladière* (onion tart). At Carnaval time, don't miss its dreamy *bugnes de Carnaval,* doughnut-like fritters delicately scented with orange blossoms. (04 93 80 92 45; www.lafougasserie.com; 5 rue de la Poissonnerie; items from €1; 7am-7pm Fri-Tue)

Olive et Artichaut

PROVENCAL €€

12 MAP P42, D4

There's barely enough room to swing a pan in this tiny street bistro, especially when it's full of diners (as it often is), but it doesn't seem to faze young Niçois chef Thomas Hubert and his friendly team. He sources as much produce as possible from close-to-home suppliers (Sisteron lamb, Niçoise olives, locally caught fish) and likes to give the old classics his own spin. Wise diners reserve. (04 89 14 97 51; www.oliveartichaut.com; 6 rue Ste-Réparate; 3-course menu €32, mains €16-28; noon-2pm & 7.30-10pm Wed-Sun)

Koko Green

VEGETARIAN €

13 MAP P42, E3

At this popular Vieux Nice new-comer, a New Zealander and a naturopath whip up an awesome array of veggie, raw and vegan treats. Weekly specials are globally inspired: Mexican *sopa de tortilla,* Middle Eastern falafel, Vietnamese crêpes – all organic, gluten-free and accompanied by fresh-blended juices. The ultimate showstopper is the vegan cheese-cake; dairy-lovers can only marvel at the faux-creaminess! (07 81 63 14 88; www.kokogreen.com; 1 rue de la Loge; weekly specials €15; noon-5pm Thu, Fri & Sun, noon-4pm & 7.30-10pm Sat;)

La Cave du Fromager

FRENCH €€

14 MAP P42, E3

Fromage is what fuels the convivial mood at this candlelit, brick- and stone-vaulted cellar bistro. The menu changes with the seasons but always revolves around cheese: Roquefort-broccoli soup; baked Camembert with hazelnuts, honey and *calvados;* hearty old-fashioned *tartiflette* (the classic Savoyard casserole of potatoes, lardons, onions and melted Reblochon cheese...). The new owners exude youthful energy and speak excellent English. (04 93 13 07 83; www.lacavedufromager.com; 29 rue Benoît Bunico; mains €18-23; 7-10pm Wed-Mon)

Acchiardo restaurant (p46)

RIVER THOMPSON/LONELY PLANET ©

Vieux Nice Eating

La P'tite Cocotte
BISTRO €€

15 🔪 MAP P42, F2

Everyone loves this intimate backstreet hideaway, named for its trademark dessert, a sinfully tasty chocolate fondant baked in a *p'tite cocotte* (mini casserole dish) and paired with pistachio ice cream. But we're getting ahead of ourselves. The whole menu abounds in creatively recombined Mediterranean ingredients: purple asparagus risotto, creamy Parmesan-lemon ravioli, or roast codfish with thyme and eggplant lasagne. Yum! (🖉 04 97 08 48 61; www.la-ptitecocotte.fr; 11 rue St-Augustin; 2-/3-course menu €24.50/29.50; ⏱noon-2.15pm Sat & Sun, 6.45-10.15pm Thu-Tue)

Drinking

La Movida
COCKTAIL BAR

16 🍷 MAP P42, E5

No place in Vieux Nice offers better people-watching than the beach-facing tables on La Movida's streetside deck and upstairs terrace. Snag one in time for sunset if you can, and stick around for cocktails, tapas, DJs and live music. (🖉 04 93 80 48 04; www.movidanice.com; 41 quai des États-Unis; ⏱10am-2am)

El Merkado
BAR

17 🍷 MAP P42, B4

Footsteps from cours Saleya, this hip tapas bar (strapline: 'In Sangria We Trust') struts its vintage stuff on

---

Ice Ice Baby: Sweet Interludes
🍽

Between sunbathing sessions on the beach, there's no sweeter interlude than a visit to one of Vieux Nice's renowned ice-cream shops.

Fenocchio (Map p42, E3; 🖉 04 93 80 72 52; www.fenocchio.fr; 2 place Rossetti; 1/2 scoops €2.50/4; ⏱9am-midnight Mar-Nov) This *maître glacier* (master ice-cream maker) has been king of the scoops since 1966. The array of flavours is mind-boggling – olive, tomato, fig, beer, lavender and violet to name a few. Dither too long over the 70-plus options and you'll never make it to the front of the queue. The wait is sometimes shorter at the **second branch** (🖉 04 93 62 88 80; www. fenocchio.fr; 6 rue de la Poissonnerie; 1/2 scoops €2.50/4; ⏱9am-midnight Wed-Mon Mar-Nov) around the corner.

Gelateria Azzurro (Map p42, D3; 🖉 04 93 13 92 24; www.facebook. com/Gelateriazzurro; 1 rue Ste-Réparate; ice cream from €2.70; ⏱11am-midnight) Yes, the ice cream here is divine, but even more exceptional are the homemade waffle cones, cooked on the hot griddle right before your eyes!

Fenocchio ice-cream shop

the ground floor of a quintessential Niçois town house. Lounging on its pavement terrace or a sofa with an after-beach cocktail is the thing to do here. (☎04 93 62 30 88; www. el-merkado.com; 12 rue St-François de Paule; ◷11am-1.30am Oct-Apr, 10am-2.30am May-Sep)

Les Distilleries Idéales CAFE

18 ⏱ MAP P42, E4

The most atmospheric spot for a tipple in the old town, whether you're after one of the many beers on tap or a local wine by the glass. Brick-lined and set out over two floors (with a little balcony that's great for people-watching), it's packed until late. Happy hour is from 6pm to 8pm. (☎04 93 62 10 66; www.facebook.com/ldinice; 24 rue de la Préfecture; ◷9am-12.30am)

Ma Nolan's PUB

19 ⏱ MAP P42, C4

This Irish pub is big, loud and *the* pub of reference for all foreigners in town (there's another branch down by the port). With live music, pub grub and Guinness on tap, it can get rowdy. (☎04 93 80 23 87, 04 26 78 07 13; www.ma-nolans.com; 2 rue St-François de Paule; ◷11am-2am; 🛜)

La Shounga COCKTAIL BAR

20 ⏱ MAP P42, G6

Decadent all-day desserts, ice-cream sundaes and cocktails (from €5) are the reason to hit the sea-facing terrace of this vibrant mojito bar. (☎04 92 27 75 93; www. shounga.bar; 12 place Guynemer; ◷8am-12.30am; 🛜)

Duelling Pasta Makers

For centuries Nice identified more with Italy than with France, and the city's deep Italian cultural roots survive in a wealth of fresh pasta shops. At rue Ste-Réparate 7, **Maison Barale** makes scrumptious ravioli stuffed with artichokes, pistachios or candied lemon; across the street, 200-year-old **Maison Tosello** is famous for its pellet-shaped chard-and-potato gnocchi known as *merda di can* (yes, dog poop!).

Snug & Cellar   PUB

21 MAP P42, E3

A more chilled retreat than many of the pubs in the old town, especially if you can bag one of the prime tables in the eponymous cellar. Weekly open mics, Sunday game nights, televised rugby and football, and occasional live bands keep the interest going. (📞09 63 08 02 12; www.facebook.com/TheSnugAndCellar; 22 rue Droite; ⏰4pm-12.30am Mon-Thu, to 2am Fri, noon-2am Sat, noon-12.30am Sun)

Entertainment

Opéra de Nice   OPERA

22 MAP P42, C4

The vintage 1885 grande dame hosts opera, ballet and orchestral concerts. (📞04 92 17 40 79; www.opera-nice.org; 4-6 rue St-François de Paule)

Shapko   LIVE MUSIC

23 MAP P42, E3

Near the cathedral square, Shapko stages live music nightly in a variety of genres: blues, funk, jazz, R&B, soul, rock and more. Happy hour runs from 6pm to 9pm. (📞06 15 10 02 52; www.shapkobar.fr; 5 rue Rossetti; ⏰6pm-2.30am)

Wayne's   LIVE MUSIC

24 MAP P42, D3

One of a strip of raucous drinking holes on the edge of the old town, Wayne's is a proper pub, through and through: plenty of beers on tap, a nightly roster of bands and big-screen sports action. This place is as scruffy as they come, but great fun if that's what you're in the mood for. (📞04 93 13 46 99; www.waynes.fr; 15 rue de la Préfecture; ⏰10am-2am)

Shopping

Maison Auer   FOOD

25 MAP P42, C4

With its gilded counters and mirrors, this opulent shop – run by the same family for five generations – looks more like a 19th-century boutique than a sweets shop, but this is where discerning Niçois have been buying their *fruits confits* (crystallised fruit) and *amandes chocolatées* (chocolate-covered almonds) since 1820. (📞04 93 85 77 98; www.maison-auer.com; 7 rue St-François de Paule; ⏰9am-6pm Tue-Sat)

Friperie Caprice

VINTAGE

26 🔒 MAP P42, E3

Nice's favourite vintage shop is a treasure trove of clothing, jewellery and accessories spanning much of the 20th century; what really sets it apart is the generous advice and assistance of amiable owner Madame Caprice, who knows every piece in the shop. (📞09 83 48 05 43; www.facebook.com/CapriceVintage Shop; 12 rue Droite; ⏱2-7pm Mon, 11am-1.30pm & 2.30-7pm Tue-Sat)

Cave de la Tour

WINE

27 🔒 MAP P42, F1

Since 1947, locals have been trusting the owners of this atmospheric *cave* (wine cellar) to find the best wines from across the Alpes-Maritimes and Var. It's a ramshackle kind of place, with upturned wine barrels and blackboard signs, and a loyal clientele, including market traders and fishmongers getting their early-morning wine fix. Lots of wines are available by the glass. (📞04 93 80 03 31; www.cavedelatour. com; 3 rue de la Tour; ⏱7am-8pm Tue-Sat, to 12.30pm Sun)

Galerie ArtNice

ART

28 🔒 MAP P42, E2

The local artwork in this Vieux Nice gallery ranges from jewellery and fashion accessories to paintings and etchings, but the catchiest souvenirs here are the miniature replicas of the famous blue chairs that line Nice's Promenade des Anglais. (📞06 07 19 00 61; www. artnice.com; 2 rue Droite; ⏱11.30am-7pm Mon-Sat)

Opéra de Nice

VICHIE81/SHUTTERSTOCK ©

Maison Auer (p52)

Olio Donato

FOOD

29 🔒 MAP P42, D3

Italian influence in Nice has always been strong, and it remains so today in shops such as Olio Donato, where you'll find a wealth of products from neighbouring Piemonte. Top draws include white truffle oil, olive oil and spectacular hazelnut spread (ask for a taste – it puts Nutella to shame!). (📞09 83 87 58 38; 5 rue de la Boucherie; ⏰10am-6.30pm)

Les Grandes Caves Caprioglio

WINE

30 🔒 MAP P42, D4

This well-stocked shop is a good place to find Bellet, a small-production AOC wine grown on the hillsides northwest of Nice. It's also where locals go to fill their own bottles with bulk wine for €1.50 per litre! (📞04 93 85 66 57; 16 rue de la Préfecture; ⏰8am-1pm & 3-7.30pm Tue-Sat, 8am-1pm Sun)

La Boutique du Flacon

PERFUME

31 🔒 MAP P42, E3

Take a trip back in time at this unique shop specialising in vintage perfume bottles with belle-époque-style spray pumps. English-speaking artist-owner Sarah Bartlett also sells crystalware, handbags, Murano jewellery, and floral essences from Grasse, France's perfume capital. (www.laboutiqueduflacon.com; 22 rue Benoît Bunico; ⏰11am-6pm)

Le Fromage CHEESE

32 🅐 MAP P42, D4

Owner Laurent Viterbo presides over a cornucopia of locally pro-duced cheeses – including sheep-, goat- and cow-milk varieties – at this favourite Vieux Nice *fromage-rie*. (📞09 51 00 19 22; www.lefromage. fr; 25 rue de la Préfecture; ☉8am-1pm & 4-7pm Tue-Sat, 8am-1pm Sun)

Pâtisserie LAC FOOD

33 🅐 MAP P42, D4

Delectable macaroons and choco-lates from *pâtissier* (pastry chef) Pascal Lac. There are three other branches around town. (📞04 93 53 60 69; www.patisseries-lac.com; 12 rue de la Préfecture; ☉9.30am-7.30pm Mon-Sat, 9.30am-1pm & 3-7pm Sun)

Moulin à Huile d'Olive Alziari FOOD

34 🅐 MAP P42, B4

Superb (but very expensive) hand-pressed olive oil, fresh from the mill on the outskirts of Nice. It comes in several flavours of differ-ing fruitiness. The shop also sells delicious tapenades, jams, honeys and other goodies. From Monday to Friday you can visit the mill to see the process in action: catch bus 3 to the Terminus stop. (📞04 93 62 94 03; www.alziari.com.fr; 14 rue St-François de Paule; ☉9am-7pm Mon-Sat, from 10am Sun)

Explore ◉

New Town & Promenade des Anglais

No neighbourhood seduces like Nice's opulent, palm-lined beachfront promenade, which has been luring tourists since the 1800s. The New Town and Promenade des Anglais are not only the heart of Nice's beach scene but also the city's commercial core, packed with hotels, restaurants and big-name shops.

Greet the day with delectable doughy treats at Mama Baker (p72), then stroll along pretty green Promenade du Paillon (p70) to the pedestrianised Carré d'Or shopping district. After a crash course in belle-époque Niçois history at Musée Masséna (p62), hit the Promenade des Anglais (p58) for a beachside lunch at Sporting Plage (p73). In the afternoon, lounge on a beach chair, take a dip or simply stroll along the promenade. Come evening, enjoy aperitifs at La Part des Anges (p75), dinner at Franchin (p71), and a nightcap at Hôtel Negresco (p70).

Getting There & Around

Walking is the most enjoyable way to explore the beachfront. Inland, trams and buses help navigate the neighbourhood's 2km-wide span.

🚋 North–south line 1 stops at the train station and place Masséna. Line 2 runs east–west, a few blocks in from the waterfront.

🚌 Several Lignes d'Azures run east–west, including lines 8, 52 and 98 along the Promenade des Anglais.

Neighbourhood Map on p68

Place Masséna (p67) KABIRK/SHUTTERSTOCK ©

Top Sight 📷
Promenade des Anglais

Nice's fabled beachfront promenade, locally nick-named La Prom, has defined the city's western waterfront for nearly 200 years – longer than Nice has belonged to France! Originally conceived in the 1820s as a 2m-wide seaside path to serve overwintering British aristocrats, it had grown by the turn of the 20th century into a gaslit, 7km-long thoroughfare and the Riviera's most prestigious address.

◎ MAP P68, C5

🚌 8, 52, 62

Vintage Hotels

The train came to Nice in 1864, prompting a ten-fold increase in the number of sun-seeking tourists. Hotels began springing up alongside villas as the Prom continued to broaden and lengthen, quickly becoming Nice's glitziest piece of real estate. Over the next 70 years, early arrivals such as the **Hôtel West End** (1842) were joined by several others still standing today, including the **Westminster** (1881), the **Royal** (1906) and the art-deco Palais de la Méditerranée (1929; p65). Perhaps most famous of all is the Hôtel Negresco (p70), whose distinctive façade and rose-hued dome continue to wow visitors, much as its central heating and private bathrooms wowed guests when it opened in 1912. This grande dame still holds court near the centre of the Promenade at No 37.

Endless Beaches

The Promenade des Anglais boasts more than a dozen named beaches between **Plage Carras** (near Côte d'Azur Airport) and **Plage du Centenaire** (opposite Jardin Albert 1er, near Vieux Nice). Most are private, visibly fenced off with their own restaurants, bars, sun loungers and umbrellas for rent. Private beaches offer several advantages: comfortable seating, greater security for your valuables, food and drink available on-site, and other perks like showers and wi-fi. Of course there's a price to pay for all these creature comforts; figure about €20 to €25 per day for a beach umbrella and lounger.

Other beaches, such as Plage du Centenaire at the eastern end of Promenade des Anglais, are free to the public, as are unfenced areas in between the private beaches – just find a patch of open space and plunk yourself down. Note that the strip of pebbles immediately adjacent to the water is also publicly accessible, allowing you to walk the entire length of the beach if you like.

★ **Top Tips**

○ Nice's private beaches charge a fee for use of their facilities; even so, you're still free to walk across them, as long as you stay close to the water and don't dawdle.

○ Many private beaches offer half-day discounts after 2pm.

○ When you cross into Vieux Nice, east of Jardin Albert 1er, the beaches continue but the waterfront avenue changes its name from Promenade des Anglais to quai des États-Unis.

✕ **Take a Break**

Grab a sidewalk table at La Femme du Boulanger (p71), 200m north of the Promenade, and snack on tartines (open-faced sandwiches) or classic bistro fare.

Soak up the sun and fine Mediterranean views along with pizza, pasta and seafood specials at beachfront Sporting Plage (p73).

New Town & Promenade des Anglais Promenade des Anglais

Fun Facts:
Chandeliers & Pebbles

👍

o If it's your first time on the Côte d'Azur, you may be surprised to see that the beach is made of pebbles. Sandy beaches aren't Nice's strength. If that's what you're after, you'll have better luck about 30km west near Antibes and Juan-les-Pins. Here in Nice, enjoy the gorgeous blue water, and be grateful for the advantages of pebbles over sand – you won't have to spend time brushing flecks off your feet!

o Nice's most iconic hotel, the Negresco (pictured), was built by Romanian hotelier Henri Negresco in 1912. It's full of colourful period details like the 5m-tall, 1-tonne Baccarat crystal chandelier in its Royal Lounge, originally commissioned by Czar Nicholas II of Russia.

One thing to be aware of is that Nice's beaches are made of pebbles, not sand. So be prepared. A folding beach mattress will be your best friend, unless you're springing for a lounge chair at one of the private beaches. And get a good pair of beach shoes, to protect your feet from bruises and burns.

Iconic Blue Chairs

One of the first things you'll notice as you stroll the Promenade is the vast collection of blue metal chairs, set out invitingly in long rows to encourage relaxation – but bundled together in groups of 20 to discourage theft! They're perfect for people-watching – some oriented towards the beach, others towards the Promenade itself. In winter, finding a seat here is a piece of cake; in summer, you may be lucky to get one. If you ever find yourself craving a miniature blue chair to take home as a souvenir, Vieux Nice's Galerie ArtNice (p53) will be happy to oblige.

Echoes of the Past

The first casino appeared on the Promenade des Anglais in 1867, but it wasn't until 1891 that the city's greatest showpiece opened its doors. The stunning **Casino de la Jetée-Promenade**, flanked by turrets, topped by a melon-shaped dome and perched on a grand wooden pier, epitomised the Promenade's seaside allure for half a century until German troops destroyed it at the end of WWII. You can still see photos of the casino in its full glory at the Musée Masséna (p62), and conjure up its memory as you gaze out to sea from the Palais de la Méditerranée to the point just offshore where it once stood. Other, darker memories lurk in this same spot – this section of the Promenade was where Nice's infamous terrorist truck driver finally came to a halt on Bastille Day 2016. On the event's anniversary, Nice residents lay flowers and release balloons to honour the victims.

Top Sight 📷
Musée Masséna

Originally built as a holiday home for Prince Victor d'Essling, this lavish belle-époque villa is one of Nice's iconic landmarks. Built between 1898 and 1901 in grand neoclassical style with an Italianate twist, it's now a fascinating museum dedicated to the history of the Riviera – taking in everything from holidaying monarchs to expat Americans, the boom of tourism and the enduring importance of Carnaval.

◉ MAP P68, C5

📞 04 93 91 19 10; 65 rue de France

museum pass 24hr/7 days €10/20

🕑 10am-6pm Wed-Mon late Jun–mid-Oct, from 11am rest of year

🚌 8, 52, 62 to Congrès/ Promenade

The Villa & Its Gardens

Entering the museum's grounds from the Promenade des Anglais beachfront, you'll immediately be struck by the grandeur of its landscaped gardens, graced with palm trees, flower beds and green lawns. The villa itself was built by the Danish architect Hans-Georg Tersling (1857–1920), who was responsible for several other important buildings during the belle époque. Buy your ticket in the mansard-roofed gatehouse at the back of the property (near rue de France), then proceed to the ground floor of the late-19th-century main building, where several original rooms preserve the villa's aristocratic look and feel.

From Napoléon to Garibaldi

A marble staircase with wrought-iron railings leads up to the 1st floor. Here you'll find a striking portrait of Nice's native son Giuseppe Garibaldi in his trademark red shirt, along with artefacts related to Napoléon, who sojourned in Nice on multiple occasions. The emperor's own death mask is here, along with Empress Josephine's embroidered cape and a mother-of-pearl tiara adorned with gold and gemstones.

Belle-Époque History & Origins of Carnaval

The museum's highlight is the upstairs suite of rooms devoted to belle-époque Nice. Vintage Carnaval posters, advertisements singing the praises of Nice's eternally mild climate, and 10-course hotel dinner menus convey the spirit of the era. Especially captivating are the images – sepia-toned 19th-century photos, a painting and an ornate scale model – of the Casino de la Jetée-Promenade, the stunning melon-domed casino that long dominated the Promenade des Anglais, before German forces laid it to waste at the end of WWII.

★ Top Tips

○ Your Musée Masséna ticket grants free access to Musée Matisse, Musée d'Art Moderne et d'Art Contemporain and several other municipal museums.

○ Ever wondered why the English call this coastline the Riviera, but the French call it the 'Blue Coast'? The French term 'Côte d'Azur' was coined in 1887 by author Stéphen Liégeard; an original copy of his book by the same title is on display here.

✕ Take a Break

For exquisitely prepared, well-priced lunch specials in a historic brasserie setting, walk five minutes east to Franchin (p71).

Sip a drink and soak up some living history in the elegant bar of the century-old Hôtel Negresco (p70) next door.

Walking Tour 🥾

Strolling the Prom

No Côte d'Azur experience compares to the storied stroll along Nice's waterfront. Elegant palm-fringed hotels and villas testify to the generations of visitors who have fallen in love with this charmed spot. In summer, the wall-to-wall collection of public and private beaches is packed with sun-worshippers of every age and nationality; even in winter, this iconic promenade feels like the beating heart of Nice.

Walk Facts

Start Hôtel Negresco
End Vieux Nice
Length 1.5km; one hour

❶ Bay of the Angels

Begin your stroll at the opulent **Hôtel Negresco** (p70), whose distinctive pink dome epitomises Nice's belle-époque splendour. After peeking in at the manicured gardens of the 19th-century Villa Masséna (p62), cross to the Promenade's seaward side. Before you stretches the magnificent Baie des Anges, named – as legend would have it – for the angels who carried Nice's patron saint, Stè-Réparate, across the Mediterranean after her 3rd-century martyrdom in Palestine.

❷ Sunloungers

All along this stretch of waterfront are private beaches, each with its own sea of sunloungers and umbrellas for rent, and many with their own restaurants. A short stroll along the Promenade brings you to the first of these, Blue Beach (www.bluebeach.fr). Others you'll pass along this walk include Sporting Plage (www.sporting plage.fr), Lido Plage (www.lido nice.com) and Ruhl Plage (www.ruhl-plage.com).

❸ Dufy Painting

Keep your eyes peeled for a **reproduction of Raoul Dufy's 1927 painting** Le Casino de la je-tée, promenade aux deux calèches posted along the promenade. The subject of the painting, an elegant domed and turreted building floating on the Mediterranean like something out of a fairy tale, sat just offshore from here for over 50 years, and was Nice's splashiest turn-of-the-century casino.

❹ Plage du Centenaire

Gaze left to see the Palais de la Méditerranée, a late-1920s hotel famous for its art-deco facade. About 200m further down on the right is **Plage du Centenaire**, one of Nice's public beaches, and among the few in France that's wheelchair-friendly, with ramps crossing to the sea, wheelchair-accessible showers and parking, and special floating wheelchairs for use in the water.

❺ La Chaise de SAB

Continue east along the waterfront, passing leafy Jardin Albert 1er on your left. Soon you'll come upon a sculpture of a gigantic blue **chair** suspended in midair. Created by artist Sabine Géraudie, La Chaise de SAB marks the eastern end of the Promenade des Anglais.

❻ Quai des États-Unis

To discover a whole extra 1km of beach, continue walking east into Vieux Nice along the beachside **quai des États-Unis** (essentially an extension of the official Promenade).

Walking Tour 🥾

New Town Family Gathering Spots

North of Vieux Nice and the beach, Nice's New Town abounds in pedestrian-friendly public spaces tailor-made for community gatherings and family fun. Everything revolves around place Masséna, the city's expansive central square, which opens into a traffic-free shopping district and a pair of inviting green parks.

Walk Facts

Start Place Masséna
End La Ronronnerie
Length 3km; 1.5 hours

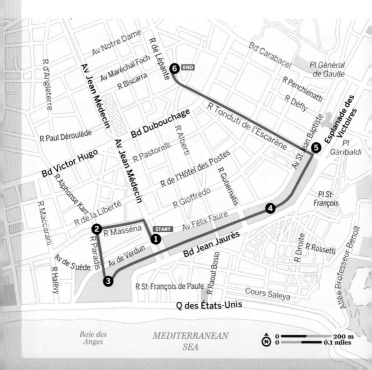

❶ Place Masséna

Nice's drawing room is this vast **plaza** adorned with colourful 19th-century buildings and checkerboard pavements that inspire kids to play spontaneous games of hopscotch. It's also the venue for Nice's midwinter Carnaval. Each year giant puppets and flower-bedecked chariots parade through the square while revellers of all ages fill the grandstands, anticipating the traditional burning of the Carnaval King.

❷ Le Carré d'Or

Nice's brand-name shopping hub, this multiblock pedestrian zone hums with energy. Niçois residents come here for anything from a new phone to a new wardrobe, and finish off with lunch or drinks at one of the dozens of sidewalk cafes. When the kids get restless, the park and the beach are both close at hand!

❸ Jardin Albert 1er

Steps from the beach, this centrally located green space is one of Nice's favourite places to celebrate, especially in July – when the Nice Jazz Festival ushers in six days of nonstop live music on two stages – and December, when the whole park is immersed in family-friendly activities such as Ferris wheel rides, ice skating and visits with Père Noël (Father Christmas).

❹ Promenade du Paillon

Once, the Paillon River ran through Nice, but it was slowly covered over by urban sprawl, including an eyesore of a bus station and parking lot. In 2013 the city replaced the concrete with this beautiful kilometre-long park, where kids now go wild playing in water jets and clambering on whimsical octopus and whale play structures.

❺ Théâtre National de Nice

A community theatre in the best sense of the word, **TNN** makes the performing arts accessible to all. Witness its Generation Z Festival, featuring live shows for families to watch together during the school holidays, or its origami, mask-making and storytelling workshops to entertain kids while their parents enjoy a night out at the theatre.

❻ La Ronronnerie

Nice kitty! What else can you say when you find yourself surrounded by five new feline friends at this cat-friendly neighbourhood cafe? Sporting pillow-topped pedestals and room-width tree-branch perches, **La Ronronnerie** (p75) encourages kitty cuddling but implores youngsters not to 'hit the cats with toys'. The result? A supremely happy family hang-out, complete with toddler-sized couch in the front window.

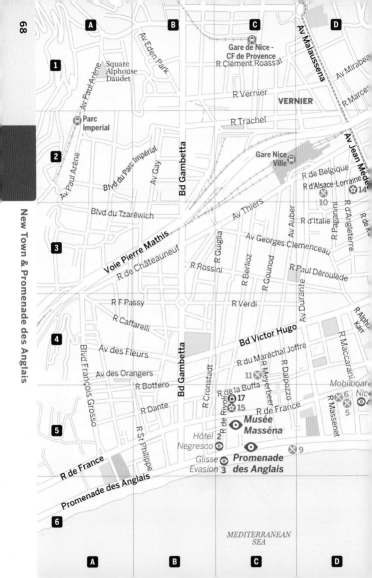

New Town & Promenade des Anglais

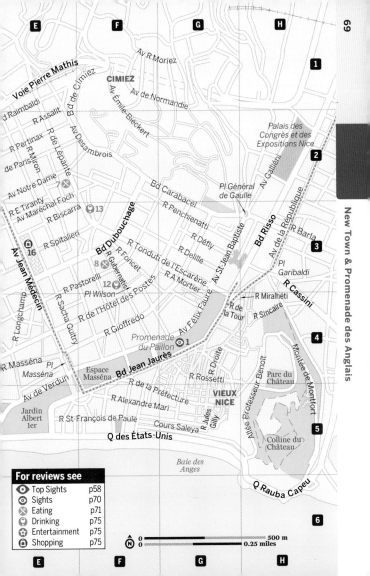

New Town & Promenade des Anglais

CIMIEZ

Av R Moriez

Voie Pierre Mathis

Bd de Cimiez

Av de Normandie

Av-Émile-Bieckert

J Raimbaldi

R Assalit

R Pertinax

de Paris

R Miron

R de Lépante

Av Decambrois

Palais des
Congrès et des
Expositions Nice

Av Gallieni

Av Notre Dame

R E Tiranty
Av Maréchal-Foch

R Biscarra

🚇13

Bd Carabacel

Pl Général
de Gaulle

R Penchienatti

Bd Risso

Av de la République

R Barla

R Spitalieri

Bd Dubouchage

R Défly

R St-Jean Baptiste

Av Jean Médecin

🚇16

8 🚇
R Guternatis

R Tonduti de l'Escarène

R Delille

Pl
Garibaldi

R Cassini

R Pastorelli

12 🚇

R Foncet

R A Mortier

R Miralhéti

R Longchamp

Pl Wilson

R de l'Hôtel des Postes

Av Félix Faure

R de
la Tour

R Sincaire

R Sacha Guitry

R Gioffredo

Promenade
du Paillon ⊙1

Montée de Montfort

R Masséna

Pl
Masséna

Espace
Masséna

Bd Jean Jaurès

R Droite

Parc du
Château

Av de Verdun

R de la Préfecture

R Rossetti

VIEUX
NICE

Allée Professeur Benoît

Jardin
Albert
1er

R Alexandre Mari

R St-François de Paule

Cours Saleya

R Jules
Gilly

Colline du
Château

Q des États-Unis

Baie des
Anges

Q Rauba Capeu

For reviews see	
⊙ Top Sights	p58
⊙ Sights	p70
✖ Eating	p71
🍷 Drinking	p75
★ Entertainment	p75
🛍 Shopping	p75

N
0 —————————— 500 m
0 —————————— 0.25 miles

E   F   G   H

Mediterranean Magnetism

Before everything else, there was the sea, and the Mediterranean climate – the twin factors that made Nice a tourist magnet as early as the 1700s. Look around and you'll find the same elemental attractions that drew Europe's belle-époque aristocrats to promenade along the waterfront in horse-drawn carriages. Even now, nothing compares to the simple joy of a balmy beach day interspersed with a spot of people-watching astride the Promenade des Anglais' famous blue chairs. Whether you're skating, kayaking, swimming, sprawled on a beach lounger or transfixed by sunset over the ever-present Med, it's all still happening by the water.

Sights

Promenade du Paillon   GARDENS

1 ◎ MAP P68, G4

It's hard to imagine that this beautifully landscaped park was once a bus station, a multistorey car park and an ill-loved square. Completed in October 2013, the park unfolds from the Théâtre National to place Masséna with a succession of green spaces, play areas and water features, and is now a favourite among Niçois for afternoon or evening strolls. (La Coulée Verte; ⏱7am-9pm Oct-Mar, to 11pm Apr-Sep; 🚊1 to Masséna, Opéra-Vieille Ville or Cathédrale-Vieille Ville)

Hôtel Negresco   LANDMARK

2 ◎ MAP P68, C5

A landmark building overlooking the grand sweep of the Promenade des Anglais, built in 1912 for Romanian innkeeper Henri Negresco. Its rosy-pink dome and lavish facade makes for a classic snapshot, but you'll need seriously deep pockets to stay here. (☎04 93 16 64 00; www.hotel-negresco-nice.com; 37 Promenade des Anglais; 🚊8, 52, 62 to Gambetta/Promenade)

Glisse Evasion   WATER SPORTS

3 ◎ MAP P68, C5

Based opposite the Hôtel Negresco, this water-sports operator has numerous methods of getting you out and about on the Med, including kayaking (€10 per hour), stand-up paddleboarding (€18 per hour), wakeboarding, waterskiing and floating around on rubber 'sofas'. Also offers paragliding (session €50). (☎06 10 27 03 91; www.glisse-evasion.com; 29 Promenade des Anglais; ⏱8.30am-7pm May-Sep; 🚊8, 52, 62 to Congrès/Promenade or Gambetta/Promenade)

Mobilboard Nice   SPORTS

4 ◎ MAP P68, D5

For an effortless cruise along Promenade des Anglais, hop

aboard an electric Segway. Rental includes a 15-minute lesson on how to ride the two-wheeled, battery-powered 'vehicle', protective helmet and audioguide. (☑04 93 80 21 27; www.mobilboard.com/nice-promenade; 2 rue Halévy, Batiment Ruhl Méridien; 30min/1hr/2hr tour €20/30/50; ⏱9.30am-6pm; ☒8, 52, 62 to Massenet)

Eating

La Femme du Boulanger

BISTRO €€

5 ⊗ MAP P68, D5

This back-alley gem with pavement seating is a vision of French bistro bliss. Mains like duck *à l'orange,* honey-balsamic glazed lamb shank, or perfect *steak au poivre* with *gratin dauphinois*

(cheesy potatoes) and perfectly tender veggies are followed up with raspberry clafoutis, tiramisu and other scrumptious desserts. Tartines on wood-fired homemade bread are the other house speciality. (☑04 89 03 43 03; www.facebook.com/femmeduboulanger; 3 rue Raffali; mains €20-25, tartines €16-22; ⏱9am-3pm & 7-11pm; ☒8, 52, 62 to Massenet)

Franchin

FRENCH €€

6 ⊗ MAP P68, D5

White linen tablecloths give this upmarket brasserie an air of formality, but the friendly service dispels any notions of stuffiness, and the food is simply divine. Don't miss the octopus salad with potatoes and chorizo (one of the best appetisers you'll find anywhere on

Promenade du Paillon

GARIFE17/SHUTTERSTOCK ©

New Town & Promenade des Anglais Eating

Le Chantecler restaurant

the Côte d'Azur), and ask about the €16 weekday specials (excellent value for money when available). (📞 04 93 87 15 74; www.franchin.fr; 10 rue Massenet; mains €24-31; ⏰noon-2pm & 7-10pm Wed-Sun; 🚌 8, 52, 62 to Massenet)

Mama Baker   BAKERY €

7 🍴 MAP P68, E2

Great bakeries abound in France, but even here, truly creative artisanal ones stand out. Witness Mama Baker, where organic grains and speciality ingredients go into a host of unique goodies. Don't miss the delectable *bouchées aux olives,* soft and crispy bite-sized bits of olive-studded cheesy dough, or *pompe à l'huile,* a semisweet roll flavoured with olive oil and orange blossoms.

(📞06 23 91 33 86; www.facebook.com/ Mamabakernice; 13 rue de Lépante; items from €2; ⏰7am-2pm & 3-7pm Mon-Fri, 7am-6pm Sat; 🚌 4 to Toselli)

Flaveur   GASTRONOMY €€€

8 🍴 MAP P68, F3

Run by brothers Gaël and Mickaël Tourteau, this small restaurant has big culinary ambitions (and a second Michelin star as of 2018). In a Zen dining room with bold fabrics and wooden platters artfully arranged on the walls, it's a haute-cuisine temple, with dishes dressed in foams, creams, reductions and snows, and presented with the precision of museum exhibits.

For the full-blown gastronomic experience, go for the seven-course tasting menu (€145). (📞04 93 62 53 95; www.restaurant-flaveur.com; 25

rue Gubernatis; 2-course lunch menus €62, 3-/4-course dinner menus €85/99; ⏱noon-2pm Tue-Fri, 7.30-10pm Tue-Sat; 🚊3, 7, 9, 27 to Pastorelli)

Sporting Plage   MEDITERRANEAN €€

9 ⊗ MAP P68, C5

Straddling a prime stretch of beachfront at the heart of the Promenade des Anglais, Sporting serves up unbeatable Mediterranean views along with pizza, pasta and seafood-focused daily specials. (☎04 93 87 18 10; www.sportingplage.fr; 25 Promenade des Anglais; mains €18-25; ⏱noon-5pm late Dec–mid-Oct; 🚊8, 52, 62 to Congrès/Promenade)

Voyageur Nissart   BISTRO €€

10 ⊗ MAP P68, D2

There's a sense of rote predictability about this checked tablecloth bistro that's been cranking out Niçois favourites for the past several decades. The good news? It still does it well, and with a smile to boot. Three fixed-price *menus* offer a chance to sample all the classics, from *petits farcis* (stuffed vegetables) to *daube niçoise* (beef stew) to lemon tart. (☎04 93 82

19 60; www.voyageurnissart.com; 19 rue d'Alsace-Lorraine; menus €18-26; ⏱noon-2.30pm & 7-10.30pm Tue-Sun; 🚊1 to Gare Thiers)

Le Canon   FRENCH €€

11 ⊗ MAP P68, C4

Elmahdi Mobarik and Sébastien Perinetti take locally sourced cuisine to the next level at this cosy neighbourhood bistro. Every farmer is listed by name on their daily-changing chalkboard menu, and the creative, beautifully presented dishes come accompanied by a fine line-up of organic wines. With only two people running the show, service can be slow, but quality more than compensates. (☎04 93 79 09 24; www.lecanon.fr; 23 rue Meyerbeer; mains €25-28; ⏱noon-2.30pm Mon, Tue, Thu & Fri, 7.30-10.30pm Mon-Fri; 🚊7, 9, 22, 27, 59, 70 to Rivoli)

Le Chantecler   GASTRONOMY €€€

Housed in a sumptuous pink Regency dining room, the two-starred Michelin restaurant at the Hôtel Negresco (see 2 ⊙ Map p68, C5), run by locally trained chef Jean-Denis Rieubland, is a once-in-a-lifetime

New Town & Promenade des Anglais Eating

Local Tips: Designer Threads & Wallet-Friendly Lunches

Shopping Locals seek out their favourite French designers on rue Alphonse Karr in the Carré d'Or.

Cheap eats Try pedestrianised rue Masséna for low-cost brasserie lunches, or rue Lépante for a less touristy neighbourhood vibe.

Carnaval in Nice

Nice's exuberant midwinter Carnaval goes back to medieval times, but its two most enduring traditions – parades of outsized papier-mâché figures, and floats decorated with local flowers – date to the belle époque, when the city began wooing well-off northerners with the promise of mild winter weather and frivolous entertainment.

Corsos (Carnaval Parades)

Evening *corsos* (parades), starting and ending in place Masséna, remain a defining element of Nice's Carnaval. The event's annually changing theme is reflected in the costumes of the gargantuan papier-mâché king and queen, and the dozen-plus floats that follow them – each measuring 12m long by 3m wide by up to 20m tall and featuring a 2-tonne framework overlaid with papier-mâché, paint, hydraulic mechanisms and electric lighting. Acrobats, stilt-walkers and flamboyantly clad dancers add to the festive, family-friendly atmosphere.

Batailles de Fleurs (Flower Competitions)

The colourful daytime parades known as *batailles de fleurs* originated in 1876, when high-society families began decorating their carriages with elegant floral motifs and competing for silk banners. Young ladies riding within would shower the crowds with locally grown flowers, helping promote the Côte d'Azur's mild climate. Modern-day *batailles* echo many elements of a century and a half ago, with splendidly dressed women tossing bunches of roses, lilies and mimosas into the crowd. Afterwards, it's delightful to wander Nice's streets surrounded by families bearing armloads of bouquets.

Incinération du Roi (Burning of the King)

Since the early days, the festivities have closed with the ceremonial burning of the Carnaval king – originally in the open Mediterranean, more recently in place Masséna. For locals, the evening's sweetest moment is the a cappella singing of Nice's civic anthem, *Nissa la Bella*.

Planning

Nice's Carnaval spans 17 days in late February, regardless of when Ash Wednesday falls. Tickets come in two categories: *tribunes* (grandstand seats), and cheaper general admission, which puts you on the streets closer to the floats. For free admission, come in costume. Prime seats sell out fast; book ahead at www.nicecarnaval.com.

experience. Each course comes with its own wine pairing chosen by the in-house sommelier. Reservations essential. (📞 04 93 16 64 10; www.hotel-negresco-nice.com; 37 Promenade des Anglais; menus €130-230, mains €45-72; ⏰7-10pm Tue-Sat; 🚌8, 52, 62 to Gambetta/Promenade)

Drinking

La Part des Anges
WINE BAR

12 🚇 MAP P68, F3

The focus at this classy wine shop–bar is organic wines – a few are sold by the glass, but the best selection is available by the bottle, served with homemade tapenades and charcuterie platters. The name means 'the Angel's Share', referring to the alcohol that evaporates as wines age. Arrive early or reserve ahead. (📞 04 93 62 69 80; www.lapartdesanges-nice.com; 17 rue Gubernatis; ⏰10am-8.30pm Mon-Thu, to midnight Fri & Sat; 🚌7, 9 to Pastorelli or Wilson)

La Ronronnerie
CAFE

13 🚇 MAP P68, F3

Kitties rule the roost at this one-of-a-kind cafe, a must for cat-lovers. Five free-range felines roam about the tables, seeking the right lap to sit in, yawning on plush pedestals or climbing the tree branch overhead. Meanwhile, humans sip hot beverages and nibble on bagels and cake. It's all squeaky clean, without a flea in sight. (📞 09 51 51 26 50; www.laronronnerie.fr; 4 rue de Lépante; ⏰11.30am-6pm Tue-Sat; 🚌4 to Sasserno)

Entertainment

La Cave Romagnan
LIVE MUSIC

14 ⭐ MAP P68, D2

Most days of the week, this place is simply a neighbourhood hang-out where locals gather for wine and conversation. But the real highlight is its Saturday-evening series of jazz performances. (📞 07 69 54 08 06; http://caveromagnan.free.fr; 22 rue d'Angleterre; ⏰10.30am-2pm & 5-9pm Mon-Fri, to 10pm Sat; 🚌1 to Gare Thiers)

Cinéma Rialto
CINEMA

15 ⭐ MAP P68, C5

Undubbed films, with French subtitles. (www.lerialto.cine.allocine.fr; 4 rue de Rivoli; 🚌7, 9, 22, 27, 59, 70 to Rivoli)

Shopping

Nice Étoile
MALL

16 🔒 MAP P68, E3

This enormous shopping mall spans a city block and hosts the usual fashion franchises. (www.nicetoile.com; 30 av Jean Médecin; ⏰10am-7.30pm Mon-Sat, 11am-7pm Sun; 🚌1 to Jean-Médecin)

Cave Rivoli
WINE

17 🔒 MAP P68, C5

This shop in the stylish Carré d'Or district carries a wide selection of French wines, including the locally produced Bellet AOC. (📞 04 93 91 09 16; www.caverivoli.com; 6 rue de Rivoli; ⏰10am-1pm & 2.30-8pm Mon-Sat, 9am-1pm Sun; 🚌7, 9, 22, 27, 59, 70 to Rivoli)

Explore ◈

Cimiez, Libération & Vernier

When you've had your fill of waterfront thrills, escape to Nice's northern neighbourhoods. The sedate hillside Cimiez district is home to two of Nice's finest art museums, along with the city's most extensive Roman ruins. Just downhill, Libération and Vernier are family-friendly quarters whose bustling market and recently renovated train station–turned–cultural centre offer a refreshingly untouristy dose of local colour.

There's no better introduction to neighbourhood life than a trip to Marché de la Libération (p91), divided into a historic covered market (p91) and a boisterous sea of street vendors near the tram tracks. Afterwards, lunch at Chez Tintin (p88), or pick up picnic supplies at Bontà Italiane (p91) and head up Cimiez hill for lunch among the Roman ruins of Les Arènes (p88). Spend the afternoon at the Matisse (p78) and Chagall (p80) museums before returning to the Rooftop 17 (p90) bar for sunset drinks, followed by dinner at La Gauloise (p89).

Getting There & Around

Hilly, sprawling and largely residential, Cimiez is best reached by bus. For other destinations, take the tram to Libération and walk.

🚊 Line 1 runs north–south along av Malausséna through the heart of Libération and Vernier.

🚌 Several Lignes d'Azur es climb the hill to Cimiez; 15 is the most useful, stopping at both the Chagall and Matisse museums.

Neighbourhood Map on p86

Roman ruins, Musée Archéologique de Nice (p87) IRISPHOTO1/SHUTTERSTOCK ©

Top Sight 📷
Musée Matisse

Housed in a radiant red villa high above town, this museum pays homage to the artistic genius of Henri Matisse (1869–1954). The wide-ranging collection spans seven decades of Matisse's work, including paintings, sculptures, paper cutouts, drawings, prints and personal objects. Adding context to the artwork, timelines trace the trajectory of Matisse's life in Nice, where he spent his last 37 years.

⊙ MAP P86, D2

www.musee-matisse-nice. org; 164 av des Arènes de Cimiez; museum pass 24hr/7 days €10/20

🕑 10am-6pm Wed-Mon late Jun–mid-Oct, from 11am rest of year

🚌 15, 17, 20, 22 to Arènes/ Musée Matisse

Early Works

To fully appreciate Matisse's journey as an artist, it's instructive to see his sombre-toned early works, painted during his formative years at the École des Beaux-Arts in Paris, when he was still taking field trips to the Louvre to copy the great masters. Don't miss his first oil painting, *Nature Morte aux Livres* (1890), a still life portraying a stack of legal tomes, created while Matisse was a 20-year-old law student (note his signature scrawled backwards across the bottom corner).

Matisse's Love Affair with Nice

Matisse came to Nice in December 1917 seeking respite from bronchitis. It rained his entire first month here – famously reducing him to painting still lifes of his umbrella and chamber pot – but when the sun emerged he was so enamoured with the Mediterranean light that he made Nice his permanent home. The museum focuses heavily on Matisse's Nice years, with works such as *Odalisque au Coffret Rouge*, painted at Matisse's studio overlooking Nice's Cours Saleya markets, and *Tempête à Nice*, depicting wind-whipped palm trees on the Promenade des Anglais.

Paper Cutouts

The museum displays an extraordinary collection of Matisse's *gouaches découpés* (paper cutouts), which he began creating in 1941 after being diagnosed with cancer. Highlights here include *Jazz* – a boldly colourful series of images depicting circus scenes, dancing figures and personal quotes from Matisse himself, first published as a 20-page art volume in the 1940s – and the exuberant floor-to-ceiling *Fleurs et Fruits* (1952–53) in the museum's atrium, originally created at Matisse's Le Régina studio just across the street.

★ **Top Tips**

o Guided museum tours in English (€6) are available Monday or Friday with advance notice (call ☎ 04 93 53 40 53).

o For stellar views of Matisse's villa from the outside, stroll the grounds of the archaeological museum next door; it's free with your Musée Matisse ticket.

o While waiting for the bus back down the hill, don't forget to ogle Le Régina, the fabulous belle-époque palace where both Queen Victoria and Matisse once lived; it's right next to the bus stop at 71 bd de Cimiez.

✕ **Take a Break**

Walk three minutes across the park for snacks, sandwiches, salads and desserts at Kiosque Jardin des Arènes (p89).

Top Sight 📷
Musée National Marc Chagall

Aficionados of Marc Chagall will be in heaven at this national museum, the world's most extensive public collection devoted to the strange, dream-like work of the Belarusian master (1887–1985). The collection spans Chagall's entire career, from early days in St Petersburg through to his final years on the Côte d'Azur. Most of the museum is devoted to Chagall's paintings, with a few works in other media including mosaic, sculpture and stained glass.

◉ MAP P86, B4

☎ 04 93 53 87 20

www.musee-chagall.fr

4 av Dr Ménard

adult/child €10/8

🕙 10am-6pm Wed-Mon
May-Oct, to 5pm Nov-Apr

🚍 15, 22 to Musée Chagall

Early Works & Auditorium

The gallery to the left of the museum's main entrance focuses on Chagall's earlier work, including his 1914 *Self-Portrait in Green* and several striking pieces with themes ranging from the circus to the artist's native city of Vitebsk. Beyond this gallery is a concert hall whose stage is flanked by floor-to-ceiling Chagall stained-glass windows in vivid blues.

Old Testament Scenes

At the centre of the collection are 12 monumental canvases depicting Old Testament scenes from Genesis and Exodus, painted between 1955 and 1968. Measuring as much as 2.5m tall and 3m wide, they include captivating renditions of *La Création de l'Homme* (The Creation of Man), *Adam et Ève Chassés du Paradis* (Adam and Eve Expelled from Paradise) and *Moïse Recevant les Tables de la Loi* (Moses Receiving the 10 Commandments), all with Chagall's trademark use of vivid colours and dreamlike imagery.

Other Works

At the western end of the museum, an entire room is devoted to *Le Cantique des Cantiques* (The Song of Songs), a sensuous five-painting series set against bold red and pink backgrounds. Closing out the exhibit is a giant mosaic designed by Chagall for the museum in 1971. Suspended above a reflecting pool, it portrays the prophet Elijah carried to Heaven in a chariot of fire, surrounded by signs of the zodiac.

★ Top Tips

o Be aware: the Musée Chagall is a national museum operated by the French government, so admission is not included with the Nice city museum pass (p144).

o Don't miss the stunning stained-glass windows in the museum's auditorium.

o Ask about English-language show times for the wonderful documentary film featuring interviews with Chagall.

o Occasional concerts are offered here by the Opéra de Nice, Orchestre Philharmonique de Nice and other top-notch musical groups.

✕ Take a Break

Across from the museum entrance, the **Café du Musée** serves snacks and light meals.

Walk 10 minutes west to La Casa di Giorgio (p89) for low-cost, family-style Italian fare.

Cimiez, Libération & Vernier Musée National Marc Chagall

Walking Tour 🥾

Exploring Cimiez Hill

Three kilometres inland from the Mediterranean, the hilly district of Cimiez began life as the ancient Roman stronghold of Cemenelum. Over time, Cimiez evolved into an elegant residential neighbourhood of villas and refined retreats, where Queen Victoria and her retinue regularly overwintered in the 1890s, and Matisse kept his last home and studio. This walk shows you all the highlights.

Walk Facts

Start Musée Matisse
End Le Régina
Length 1.5km; one hour

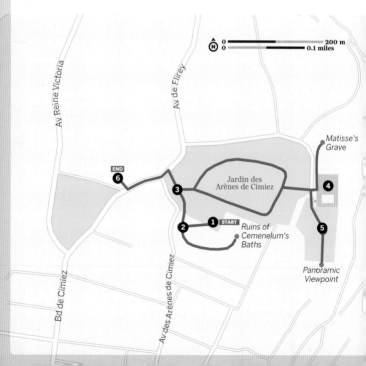

❶ Genoese Hilltop Villa

Begin your walk outside the **Musée Matisse** (p78), housed in the beautiful Palais de Gubernatis, a Genoese-style villa dating to 1685. Gazing up at the rust-red walls and chartreuse shutters, take a moment to study the ornate 'stone' window frames. Notice anything funny? They're trompe l'œil imitations painted onto the plaster.

❷ Roman Baths

Walk a few paces southwest to the Musée Archéologique de Nice (p87) and cross the lobby to reach the back garden (free admission with a Musée Matisse ticket). You're now standing in the heart of ancient Cemenelum, the 1st- to 4th-century AD Roman city whose name survives as Cimiez. Wander east through the rubble for photogenic views of the Matisse Museum and the impressive ruins of Cemenelum's **baths**, their arched white stone walls striped with red brick.

❸ Olive Groves & Ancient Ruins

Return through the museum entrance and continue north to the spectral vestiges of **Les Arènes** (p88), Cemenelum's 5000-seat amphitheatre. The ruins here may be...well, ruined – but they provide a scenic backdrop for the old men playing pétanque (boules) on the adjacent courts. From here, stroll east through the Jardin des Arènes

de Cimiez, a lovely green park dotted with ancient olive trees that makes a perfect picnic spot.

❹ Matisse's Final Resting Place

Continue across the road to the Monastère Notre Dame de Cimiez (p87), whose 15th-century church sits surrounded by beautiful gardens. Turn left and pass through a gate into the cemetery, then follow signs around to the left again and downhill to **Matisse's grave**, an unadorned, flat stone slab that seems out of keeping with the artist's proclivity for whimsical lines and bold colours.

❺ Monastery Garden

Head back to the front of the church, then south through the **Jardin du Monastère** (monastery garden) to a panoramic viewpoint with lovely perspectives on Nice and the distant Mediterranean.

❻ Queen Victoria's Winter Retreat

From here retrace your steps through the olive trees and exit the park onto bd de Cimiez. Beside the bus stop (where you can catch bus 15 for Musée National Marc Chagall), pause to contemplate **Le Régina** (p88), the monumental palace-turned-apartment building where Queen Victoria wintered in the 1890s and Matisse lived half a century later.

Walking Tour 🚶

A Morning in Libération

Ask Nice residents to name their favourite neighbourhoods, and Libération inevitably makes the list. Nice's tram line, which runs down central av Malausséna, has prompted an influx of new residents and community-based development projects. Today it's an up-and-coming, family-friendly place with a vibrant ethnic and religious mix, brimming with street life and renovated 19th-century buildings – yet largely off the tourist radar.

Walk Facts

Start Kiosque Chez Tintin
End Gare du Sud
Length 1km; 30 minutes

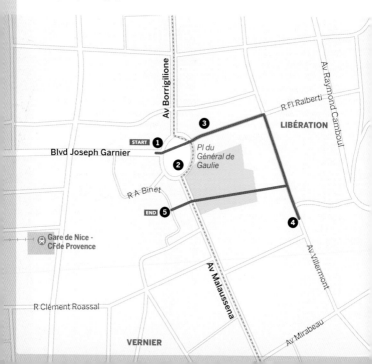

❶ Kiosque Chez Tintin

Early risers start their day at this friendly **kiosk** (p88) near the edge of Libération's open-air market, stopping in for a *café* (espresso) or a *noisette* (espresso with a dab of steamed milk). Tintin is also everybody's favourite spot for *pan bagnat*, the quintessential Niçois sandwich of tuna, olives, hard-boiled eggs and assorted veggies piled onto an olive-oil-slathered roll.

❷ Marché de la Libération

After Vieux Nice's Cours Selaya food market, this outdoor venue centred around Libération's place du Général de Gaulle is the largest produce **market** (p91) in Nice. Market gardeners display piles of fruit, veggies, flowers, honey, cheeses and other local products. Stalls run parallel to the tram tracks for two or three blocks and spill over into side streets such as rue Clément Roassal.

❸ Cité Marchande Docks de la Riviera

Neighbourhood residents hobnob with the butcher, the fishmonger and the cheese merchant while planning their evening menu at this popular **covered market** (p91). The entryway is easy to miss amid the colourful profusion of sidewalk fruit vendors out front.

❹ Brasserie Artisanale de Nice

For an emblematic Libération experience, stop in at this beloved backstreet **nanobrewery** (p90), locally famous for its chickpea-based Zytha beer. Owner Oliver Cautain's passion is palpable as he describes his hands-on, small-batch approach: buying raw materials locally and doing everything from milling malt to stickering bottles by hand. For a taste of Cautain's latest brews, plan ahead, as hours are limited.

❺ Gare du Sud

Inaugurated in 1892, Libération's grand old **train station** (p88) dispatched narrow-gauge trains through the palm trees into the Alps for nearly a century. Nearly razed in favour of 1990s apartment blocks, it's now a national historic monument housing Libération's sparkling new community centre, complete with library, cinema and a slew of cafes and restaurants scheduled to move in by 2020.

Cimiez, Libération & Vernier

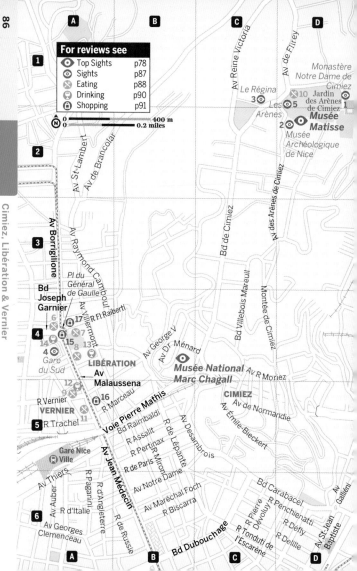

For reviews see

⊙	Top Sights	p78
⊙	Sights	p87
⊗	Eating	p88
🍸	Drinking	p90
🛍	Shopping	p91

0 — 400 m
0 — 0.2 miles

Av Reine Victoria

Av de Flirey

Monastère Notre Dame de Cimiez

Le Régina

⊙3 Les Arènes

⊗10 Jardin des Arènes de Cimiez 1

⊙5

2⊙⊙ Musée Matisse

Musée Archéologique de Nice

Av St-Lambert

Av de Brancolar

Av Borriglione

Av Raymond Comboul

Pl du Général de Gaulle

Bd Joseph Garnier

⊗6 ⊙17

Av Villermont

Av Fl Raiberti

⊗14 ⊙15

⊗8 ⊙13

⊙7

4⊙ Gare du Sud

LIBÉRATION
Av Malaussena

Av George V

Av Dr Ménard

Bd de Cimiez

Bd Villebois Mareuil

Montée de Cimiez

Av des Arènes de Cimiez

Musée National Marc Chagall

Av R Moriez

CIMIEZ

Av de Normandie

⊗12

⊙16 R Marceau

Voie Pierre Mathis

VERNIER

⊗11 R Vernier

R Trachel

Av Émile-Bieckert

Gare Nice Ville

Bd Raimbaldi

R Assalit

R Pertinax

R de Lépante

R Miron

Av Desambrois

R de Paris

R Notre Dame

Av Jean Médecin

Av Notre Dame

Av Maréchal Foch

R Biscarra

Bd Carabacel

R Pierre Devoluy

R Penchienatti

R Défly

R Delille

Av Auber

Av Thiers

R Paganini

R d'Angleterre

R de Russie

Av St Jean Baptiste

Av Galliéni

Av Georges Clemenceau

R d'Italie

R Tonduti de l'Escarène

Bd Dubouchage

Sights

Monastère Notre Dame de Cimiez

MONASTERY

1 ⊙ MAP P86, D1

Painters Henri Matisse and Raoul Dufy are buried in the cemetery of this monastery, a five-minute walk across the park from the Musée Matisse. To reach **Matisse's grave**, turn left after crossing through the gate and weave through the grandiose family plots down to the lower cemetery, where you'll find a flat stone monument engraved with the names of the artist and his wife, Amélie. (place du Monastère; ⏰8.30am-12.30pm & 2.30-6.30pm; 🚌15, 17, 20, 22 to Arènes/Musée Matisse)

Musée Archéologique de Nice

MUSEUM

2 ⊙ MAP P86, D2

The hodgepodge of Roman artefacts in this archaeological museum is rather ho-hum – but if you've already bought a Nice museum pass, it's worth a visit just to wander the grounds, which afford some lovely views of Matisse's villa and the adjacent Roman baths, all backed by rows of cypress trees. (📞04 93 81 59 57; www.nice.fr/fr/culture/musees-et-galeries; 160 av des Arènes; museum pass 24hr/7 days €10/20; ⏰10am-6pm Wed-Mon late Jun–mid-Oct, from 11am rest of year; 🚌15, 17, 20 or 22 to Arènes/Musée Matisse)

Monastère Notre Dame de Cimiez

Scenic Railway into the Alpine Foothills

Nice's idyllic mountainous hinterland is closer than you think, and there's no easier or more enjoyable way to get there than on the scenic **Train des Pignes** (Pine Cone Train; www.trainprovence.com; single/return Nice to Digne €24.10/48.20; 🚊1 to Libération). This historic narrow-gauge railway takes you through river gorges, past hilltop villages and up into the rugged foothills of the Alps, all within an easy day trip of Nice. The train leaves from **Gare de Nice-CF de Provence** (rue Alfred Binet; 🚊1 to Libération), a five-minute walk west of the Libération tram stop.

Ride the rails all the way to Digne-les-Bains, or hop off wherever you like and catch the next train down the mountain whenever you're ready. The beautiful medieval village of **Entrevaux,** just 1½ hours from Nice (return fare €24.40) makes a particularly nice spot for lunch and a wander through its historic centre and citadel.

Le Régina
HISTORIC BUILDING

3 ⊙ MAP P86, C1

Originally Queen Victoria's wintering palace, this monumental edifice was subsequently converted into apartments. In the 1940s Matisse lived here, using one unit as a studio and another as his home, and it was here that the artist died in 1954. Visitors can admire the building from the outside while waiting for a bus downhill from the Matisse Museum. (71 bd de Cimiez; 🚌15, 17, 20 or 22 to Arènes/Musée Matisse)

Gare du Sud
HISTORIC BUILDING

4 ⊙ MAP P86, A4

This cool old 19th-century railway station was originally built to provide train service from Nice into the Alps. A century later, when it was replaced by the nearby Gare de Provence, it was threatened with demolition, but the community stepped in to save it. Now it's the site of a new library and a multiplex movie theatre, and a food court scheduled to open by 2020. (place de la Gare du Sud; 🚊1 to Libération)

Les Arènes
RUINS

5 ⊙ MAP P86, D1

The scant remains of Nice's Roman amphitheatre can't compare to other ancient sites in France, but they do lend an atmospheric air to the park outside the Musée Matisse. (blvd de Cimiez; admission free; 🚌15, 17, 20 or 22 to Arènes/Musée Matisse)

Eating

Kiosque Chez Tintin
SANDWICHES €

6 ❌ MAP P86, A4

A true local institution, this friendly little kiosk makes some of Nice's best *pan bagnat*. Locals flock here before or after a visit to the nearby Libération market. (☎04 92 09 16 19; www.facebook.com/kiosquetintin; 3 pl du Général de Gaulle; sandwiches €5; ⏰6am-3pm Tue-Sun; 🚊1 to Libération)

La Casa di Giorgio   ITALIAN €

7 🍴 MAP P86, A4

Don't let Giorgio's informal mom-and-pop vibe fool you! Snagging a table requires serious planning. With low prices, friendly service, tasty homemade pasta, and quarter-litre carafes of local wine going for €4.50, it books up fast even in low season. Bottom line: you won't find a more affordable sit-down lunch anywhere in Nice. (☎06 89 20 50 35; 2 rue Flaminius Raiberti; mains €8-14; ⏰8am-3.30pm Mon-Sat; 🚊1 to Libération)

La Table d'Etsuko   JAPANESE €€

Market-fresh cuisine takes on new meaning at this lovely *table d'hôte* (home kitchen serving meals). Three times a week, Japanese chef Etsuko invites up to eight guests to her apartment near the Libération market for healthy, delicious lunches built around fresh fish and organic vegetables. Reserve ahead, when you'll be given the location. (www.facebook.com/latabledetsuko; lunch €20; ⏰12.15-1.30pm Tue-Thu; 🚊1 to Libération)

La Gauloise   BRASSERIE €€

8 🍴 MAP P86, A4

With red and black booths and lashings of exposed brick, this cheerful place in the heart of the Libération neighbourhood serves up solid brasserie food in a lively setting. Go for appetisers such as *beignets de crevettes* (shrimp fritters), followed by lamb chops grilled with thyme, or ravioli with *pistou* sauce. Service is friendly and everything is dependably homemade. (☎04 93 62 07 90; www.restaurant-lagauloise.fr; 28 av Malausséna; mains €14-24; ⏰9am-11pm Tue-Sat, to 3pm Sun; 🚊1 to Libération)

Au Petit Libanais   LEBANESE €

9 🍴 MAP P86, A5

This family-run Lebanese place offers a delicious break from Nice's ubiquitous French and Italian fare. Platters of marinated and grilled meat (kafta, shawarma etc) come accompanied by sides of hummus, tabouleh and more – all at very wallet-friendly prices. (☎04 93 81 33 03; 2 rue Vernier; mains €12-16; ⏰noon-3pm & 6.30-11pm Mon-Sat; 🚊1 to Libération)

Kiosque Jardin des Arènes   SANDWICHES €

10 🍴 MAP P86, D1

The lone eatery near the Musée Matisse is this humble parkside kiosk, serving panini, salads and Niçois specialities such as *pan bagnat*, *tourte de blette* (chard pie) and *pissaladière* (caramelised onion tart) – followed up with apple or lemon tart, and waffles with Nutella and whipped cream. (Jardin des Arènes de Cimiez;

snacks €2.50-7.50; ☺11am-6pm; 🚌15, 17, 20 or 22 to Arènes/Musée Matisse)

Arlequin Gelati   ICE CREAM

11 🚫 MAP P86, A5

A five-minute walk from Nice Ville train station brings you to this fab ice-cream shop founded by Milanese gelato master Roberto. Grab a scoop of chocolate-orange, hazelnut, pistachio, panna cotta or cinnamon-infused *spéculoos,* take it to the pavement tables out the front, and watch the world go by. (📞04 93 04 69 88; www.arlequin-gelati.com; 9 av Malausséna; 1/2/3/4 scoops €3/5/7/9; ☺10am-midnight Apr–mid-Oct; 👶; 🚋1 to Libération or Gare Thiers)

Drinking

Rooftop 17   BAR

12 🍸 MAP P86, A5

Panoramic 360-degree views of Nice are the big draw at the Hôtel Monsigny's rooftop bar. Glasses of rosé, mojitos and fresh fruit smoothies all go down well on the comfortable armchairs and sofas spread across the sunny deck. Reserve ahead, especially for sunset, when the place gets packed. (📞04 93 88 27 35; www.hotelmonsignynice.com; 17 av Malausséna; ☺10.30am-11pm; 🚋1 to Libération)

Brasserie Artisanale de Nice   BREWERY

13 🍺 MAP P86, A4

Taste some of southern France's most interesting beers at this neighbourhood microbrewery, which opens to the public a few hours per week. Don't miss the flagship Zytha, a Niçois classic brewed with chickpeas, or the Blùna, made with bitter-orange peel and coriander. (📞09 73 59 20 30; www.brasserie-nice.com; 14 av Villermont; 5-7pm Tue-Fri, 10am-noon & 4-7pm Sat; 🚋1 to Libération)

Local Experiences:
Butcher's Banter & Sunset Views   🔭

Jardin des Arènes Cimiez' hilltop park (Map p86, D1), is a favourite local hang-out where old folks play *pétanque* (boules) among the olive groves and Roman ruins, and families flock for traditional Niçois festivals like Festin des Cougourdons in March and Lu Festin de Nissa in May.

Markets Banter with the butcher and find your favourite sheep's-milk cheese at the covered **Marché de la Libération**, or plan your picnic at the fruit and veggie stands just outside.

Eating and drinking spots Greet the day with coffee and *pan bagnat* at ever-popular **Kiosque Chez Tintin** (p88), or savour sunset views over cocktails and tapas at **Rooftop 17**.

L'Altra Casa CAFE

14 MAP P86, A4

Libération's go-to bar-cafe for morning coffee and afternoon aperitifs is always buzzing, especially in summer, when tables are spread out on the big square between the market and the old train station. (04 89 97 06 93; www.facebook.com/latracasanice; 2 place de la Gare du Sud; 5.45am-11pm Tue-Fri, to 3.30pm Sat, to 1pm Sun; 1 to Libération)

Shopping

Marché de la Libération MARKET

15 MAP P86, A4

After the Cours Selaya produce market, this is Nice's largest outdoor display of fresh fruit and veggies – and an authentically local experience. When it's in full swing, its dozens of stalls fill several city blocks along av Malaussèna, place du Général de Gaulle, place de la Gare du Sud, rue Clément Roassal, rue Veillon and bd Joseph Garnier. (place du Général de Gaulle; 6am-12.30pm Tue-Sun; 1 to Libération)

Bontà Italiane FOOD & DRINKS

16 MAP P86, A5

If your taste-buds are pining for Italy, this deli is the answer to your prayers. You'll find a vast array of Italian specialities, from fresh pasta to panettone and mozzarella

Pétanque court

to mortadella, all accompanied by a good selection of wines and olive oils. (04 93 62 21 61; 10 av Malaussèna; 8.30am-1pm & 3.30-7.30pm Tue-Sat, 8.30am-12.30pm Sun; 1 to Libération or Gare Thiers)

Cité Marchande Docks de la Riviera FOOD

17 MAP P86, A4

One of Nice's most traditional covered markets is this local-focused indoor affair in a brick building near the heart of Libération. Meat, fish, cheese, charcuterie and produce are all on offer at the two-dozen stalls. (rue Flaminius Raiberti; 7am-12.30pm Tue-Sun; 1 to Libération)

Explore ✦

Le Port-Garibaldi

You couldn't ask for a lovelier Mediterranean photo op than the bobbing rows of boats in Nice's port, backed by the columned façade of Notre-Dame du Port and the Alpine foothills. This animated, easily walkable neighbourhood is beloved among locals for its vibrant social scene, with an impressive concentration of restaurants, bars and nightlife packed into a very few blocks.

The perfect morning here begins with coffee at Workhouse Café (p103) or fresh-squeezed juice at Badaboom (p101), followed by a visit to the sprawling multilevel Musée d'Art Moderne et d'Art Contemporain (p94). Stop for lunch at l'Uzine (p102), then enjoy a walk around Port Lympia (p99), punctuated by a boat cruise with Trans Côte d'Azur (p100), a spot of antique-browsing at Village Ségurane (p105) or late-afternoon beers at a sidewalk pub on the port's sunny eastern side. Return towards place Garibaldi (p99) for dinner at Café Paulette (p100), followed by a spirited evening of bar-hopping along rue Bonaparte.

Getting There & Around

The neighbourhood's main shopping, eating and drinking venues are all an easy walk from place Garibaldi or the port.

🚊 Line 1 stops at place Garibaldi. Line 2 stops at Garibaldi Le Château (under place Garibaldi) and Port Lympia (near the ferry docks).

🚌 Numerous Lignes d'Azur es serve the port area, including lines 7, 14, 20, 30 and 81.

Neighbourhood Map on p98

Nice's port EQROY/SHUTTERSTOCK ©

Top Sight 📷

MAMAC

The École de Nice, which sprang up here in the 1950s, had a significant impact on the evolution of 20th-century modern art. The impressive Musée d'Art Moderne et d'Art Contemporain (MAMAC) showcases works from various movements that took root in Nice, including nouveau réalisme, Fluxus and Supports/Surfaces, alongside pop-art classics and regularly rotating contemporary-art exhibits, all housed in a jarringly modernistic building.

◎ MAP P98, A2

www.mamac-nice.org

place Yves Klein

museum pass 24hr/7 days €10/20

🕐 10am-6pm Tue-Sun late Jun–mid-Oct, from 11am rest of year

🚊 1 to Garibaldi

Audacious Architecture

Love it or loathe it, MAMAC's architecture is undeniably striking. The museum's four blocky towers, faced in white Carrara marble, are connected by a series of glassed-in passageways, with concentric rainbow-hued patterns adding splashes of colour to the hexagonal interior courtyard overlooking central place Yves Klein. Architects Yves Bayard and Henri Vidal designed the building, which was inaugurated in 1990.

Permanent Collection

The museum's middle floors are dedicated to its exceptional permanent collection featuring artists from the École de Nice. Especially well represented is the *nouveau réalisme* of Yves Klein, with his characteristic works in bold blue, and Niki de Saint Phalle, whose eye-catching works include altars, *Nanas* (exuberantly colourful sculptures of women) and *Tirs* ('shooting paintings' created by shooting a gun at bags of paint suspended over plaster-covered surfaces). A who's-who of other Nice artists is represented, including Arman, César, Martial Raysse and Ben Vautier; don't miss the latter's *Cambra de Ben*, a smile-inducing room plastered floor to ceiling with quotes from the artist and repurposed objects. Complementing these home-grown works are pop-art pieces from Andy Warhol, Robert Indiana, Roy Lichtenstein and others.

Panoramic Terraces

For 360-degree views of Nice's skyline, climb to the museum's top level. Straddling the crossroads between Vieux Nice, the port, the Promenade du Paillon and the New Town, the rooftop's panoramic terraces command unparalleled, all-embracing city perspectives. Yves Klein's *Mur de Feu*, an assemblage of gas burners that creates hypnotic patterns when lit, adds a magical touch during special evening events.

★ Top Tips

o Guided tours (€6) take place Fridays at 3pm.

o Save time to visit the rooftop terraces for unparalleled views of Nice.

o Want to see Nice's weirdest building? Head 250m north of the museum to *La Tête Carrée*, designed by local artist Sacha Sosno.

✗ Take a Break

Recharge with a great cup of coffee at Workhouse Café (p103), just across the street.

Linger over lunch at Déli Bo (p101), or skip straight to its tempting line-up of cakes and desserts.

Walking Tour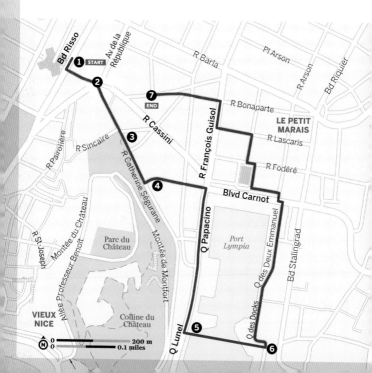

Place Garibaldi to the Port & Back

Ask a local what defines Nice's port district today, and they'll point to its bohemian quality: a bustling bar scene, quirky shops and a vibrant gay community. Yet reminders of Nice's past also abound, from 18th-century merchants' warehouses to the former galley slaves' prison, recently converted to an art gallery.

Walk Facts

Start Workhouse Café
End Rue Bonaparte
Length 2km; one hour

❶ Workhouse Café

Where do enterprising young Niçois look for office space? At this cool new 'coworking' community across from Nice's modern art museum. Stop in for breakfast at the **cafe** (p103) downstairs, where giant blackboards announce monthly rental rates and daily specials.

❷ Place Garibaldi

Surrounded by grand palaces with trompe l'œil window frames and shutters, this vast 18th-century **square** (p99) was originally a military parade ground. Now it's the neighbourhood's heart and soul, with restaurants, cafes, a cinema and two tram stops, including the new subterranean station set to open in 2019. During excavation, workers discovered ruins which may date to ancient Greek Nikaïa.

❸ Chez Fabienne Ambrosio

Family-run for generations, this neighbourhood household goods **shop** (📱04 93 14 40 43; 8 rue Catherine Ségurane; 🕙10am–noon & 2-6pm Mon-Fri) is where you'd go to buy a pan for cooking *socca*. Owner Fabienne points proudly to photos of her grandmother, who opened the place in 1935, and whose recipes for Niçoise olives and orange wine she still shares with customers.

❹ Le Quartier des Antiquaires

As you wander towards the port, you'll find over 100 **antiques**
shops squeezed into this neighbourhood's backstreets, most concentrated along rues Antoine Gautier, Catherine Ségurane and Emmanuel Philibert. For a list, see http://nice-antic.com/antiquaires.

❺ Lou Passagin

Here's your chance to travel aboard a *pointu*, the traditional pointy-nosed fishing boat of the Côte d'Azur. A living piece of maritime history, this nifty summer-only **ferry** (quai Lunel; 🕙10am-7pm mid-May–Sep; 🚊2 to Port Lympia) whisks passengers across Nice's harbour for free, five passengers at a time.

❻ Galerie Lympia

In 2017 the regional government of Alpes-Maritimes launched this innovative **gallery** (p99) inside a converted *galère* (galley slaves' prison). Exhibits, set up alongside former prisoners' bunks, alternate between avant-garde Niçois artists such as Patrick Moya and internationally renowned painters and sculptors.

❼ Rue Bonaparte

Napoléon lived here for nine months in 1794: that's what the plaque at **6 rue Bonaparte** proclaims; and the emperor would doubtless be kicking up his heels today on Le Port-Garibaldi's liveliest street, where every other doorway seems to hide a bar, a cafe or a restaurant.

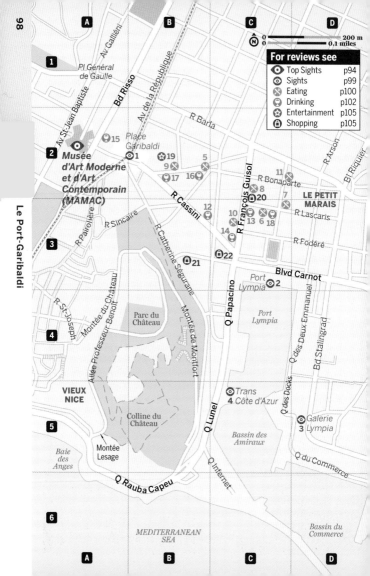

Le Port-Garibaldi

For reviews see

⊙	Top Sights	p94
⊙	Sights	p99
✖	Eating	p100
🖫	Drinking	p102
✦	Entertainment	p105
🛍	Shopping	p105

Pl Général de Gaulle

Av Gallieni

Bd Risso

Av de la République

R Barla

R Arson

Bl Riquier

15

Place Garibaldi

1

Musée d'Art Moderne et d'Art Contemporain (MAMAC)

19
9
17
16

5

11

R Bonaparte

7

LE PETIT MARAIS

R Cassini

R Pairolière

R Sincaire

R Catherine Ségurane

12

R François Guisol

8
20

10
13 6 18

14

R Lascaris

R Fodéré

21

22

Port Lympia

2

Blvd Carnot

Port Lympia

Montée du Château

Parc du Château

Montée de Montfort

Q Papacino

R St-Joseph

Allée Professeur Benoît

VIEUX NICE

Colline du Château

Montée Lesage

Q Lunel

Q Internet

Q des Deux Emmanuel

Bd Stalingrad

Trans Côte d'Azur
4

Q des Docks

Galerie Lympia
3

Baie des Anges

Bassin des Amiraux

Q du Commerce

Q Rauba Capeu

MEDITERRANEAN SEA

Bassin du Commerce

0   200 m
0   0.1 miles

Sights

Place Garibaldi SQUARE

1 MAP P98, B2

Named for Nice-born Italian nationalist and military hero Giuseppe Garibaldi, this grand square was a military parade ground at the time of its creation in the late 18th century. These days it's a major tram intersection and community gathering place, surrounded by cafes, bars and restaurants. (place Garibaldi; 1 to Garibaldi)

Port Lympia ARCHITECTURE

2 MAP P98, C3

Nice's Port Lympia, with its beautiful Venetian-coloured buildings, is often overlooked. But a stroll along its quays is lovely, as is the walk

to get here: come down through Parc du Château or follow quai Rauba Capeu, where a massive **war memorial** hewn from the rock commemorates the 4000 Niçois who died in both world wars. (2 to Port Lympia)

Galerie Lympia GALLERY

3 MAP P98, D5

Nice's coolest new gallery space is housed in this former galley slaves' prison down by the port. Opened in 2017 by the Alpes-Maritimes' departmental government after a €2.1-million restoration project, it hosts regular free exhibitions of works by Niçois artists such as Patrick Moya, along with artists from further afield. (04 89 04 53 10; http://galerielympia.departement 06.fr; 52 bd Stalingrad; admission free;

Port Lympia

Socca (chickpea-flour pancake), Chez Pipo restaurant

⊘2-7pm Wed-Sat, 10am-noon & 2-7pm Sun; 🚊2 to Port Lympia)

Trans Côte d'Azur
BOATING

4 ◎ MAP P98, C5

Trans Côte d'Azur runs one-hour boat cruises along the Baie des Anges and Rade de Villefranche (adult/child €18/13) from April to October. From late May to September it also sails to Île Ste-Marguerite (€40/31, one hour), St-Tropez (€65/51, 2½ hours), Monaco (€38.50/30, 45 minutes) and Cannes (€40/31, one hour). (www.trans-cote-azur.com; quai Lunel; ⊘Apr-Oct; 🚊2 to Port Lympia)

Eating

Café Paulette
TAPAS €€

5 🍴 MAP P98, B2

Chilled and classy Café Paulette has become one of the Petit Marais's favourite hang-outs since opening in 2017. Part cafe, part convivial lunch spot and part evening wine bar, it's especially beloved for its tasty international tapas such as roast squid and barley 'risotto' or Japanese-style sesame-crusted tuna tataki. An ample array of cocktails supplements the solid wine list. (📞04 92 04 74 48; 15 rue Bonaparte; tapas €6-10, mains €11-29; ⊘8am-12.30am Wed-Sat; 🚊1 to Garibaldi)

Jan

GASTRONOMY €€€

6 ⊗ MAP P98, C3

For the full-blown fine-dining experience, make a pilgrimage to the Michelin-starred restaurant of South African chef Jan Hendrik van der Westhuizen. Dishes here are laced with Antipodean and New World flavours, and crackle with artistic and culinary flair. There's nothing à la carte – Jan decides his *menus* on the day. It's high-end (dress smart) and sought after; reservations essential. (📞 04 97 19 32 23; www.restaurantjan.com; 12 rue Lascaris; 3-course lunch menus €55, dinner menus €98-118, incl wine pairings €137-164; ⏰7-10pm Tue-Sat, noon-2pm Fri & Sat; 🚋1 to Garibaldi, 2 to Port Lympia)

Chez Pipo

FRENCH €

7 ⊗ MAP P98, C3

Everyone says the best *socca* (chickpea-flour pancakes) can be found in the old town, but don't believe them – this place near Port Lympia has been in the biz since 1923 and, for our money, knocks *socca*-shaped spots off anywhere else in Nice. (📞04 93 55 88 82; www.chezpipo.fr; 13 rue Bavastro; socca €2.90; ⏰11.30am-2.30pm & 5.30-10pm Wed-Sun; 🚋1 to Garibaldi, 2 to Port Lympia)

Badaboom

VEGAN €

8 ⊗ MAP P98, C2

Vegans and vegetarians are in heaven at this little cafe specialising in fresh cold-pressed juices, whole grains, local organic produce and raw desserts. The menu features salads, wraps and daily *plats du jour,* each served with juice for an extra €3. (📞06 71 48 24 01; www.badaboom-nice.net; 11 rue François Guisol; plat du jour €14, with juice €17; ⏰8.30am-6pm Mon-Wed, to 10pm Thu & Fri, 10am-5pm Sat; 🖋; 🚋1 to Garibaldi, 2 to Port Lympia)

Déli Bo

CAFE €

9 ⊗ MAP P98, B2

This hybrid coffee shop–bistro is a perennially popular hang-out for discerning Niçois hipsters. It's good for bagel sandwiches, lunchtime salads and other light bites, but it's the sumptuous cakes

Windows on History

As you wander near the port, keep an eye out for signs of the neighbourhood's history. Many places down here, such as the Hierro Desvilles building at 4 rue Antoine Gautier, still retain the extra-wide doors and teeny superimposed inspector's windows used in the 19th century when goods were delivered to the port by horse-drawn cart; others have deep basements carved into the native calcareous stone, handy for warehousing large supplies of merchandise.

and superb coffee that ensures it's always packed. It does a great Sunday brunch too. (📞04 93 56 33 04; 5 rue Bonaparte; mains €7-19; ⏰7am-7pm Mon-Sat, 10am-5pm Sun; 🚊1 to Garibaldi)

Maison Gusto

MEDITERRANEAN €€

At this serious mozzarella-lover's bar (see 6 🔀 Map p98, C3), tasting platters of burrata, stracciatella, mozzarella di bufala, charcuterie and salad can keep you busy all night long. On the other hand, if you'd prefer a burger, grilled porcini mushrooms, truffle risotto, or a veal cutlet simmered in white wine, it's got that too. Either way, it's one of the neighbourhood's hottest new dinner spots. (📞04 93 07 28 68; www.maisongusto.fr; 12 rue Lascaris; mains €14-29; ⏰7-11pm Mon-Sat; 🚊1 to Garibaldi, 2 to Port Lympia)

L'Uzine

MEDITERRANEAN €€

10 🔀 MAP P98, C3

The pop-art prints and artfully distressed decor set the tone at this hip little Port Lympia place (the name means 'The Factory'), which is equally popular for weekend drinks as for its bistro food. There are bands at the weekend and a predictably trendy clientele. (📞04 93 56 42 39; 18 rue François Guisol; mains €14-32, lunch menus €18; ⏰noon-2pm & 7-10.30pm Tue-Sat; 🚊2 to Port Lympia)

Socca d'Or

FAST FOOD

11 🔀 MAP P98, C2

Locals swear by the authentic Niçois specialities served at this low-key neighbourhood eatery: *pan bagnat* (southern France's iconic tuna sandwich) on fresh homemade bread, *tourte de blette sucrée* (sweet Swiss chard tart), *pissaladière* (onion tart), *salade niçoise* and, of course, the restaurant's famous namesake *socca* (savoury chickpea pancakes). (📞04 93 56 52 93; www.restaurant-soccador-nice.fr; 45 rue Bonaparte; socca €3; ⏰11am-2pm & 6-10pm Mon, Tue & Thu-Sat; 🚊1 to Garibaldi, 2 to Port Lympia)

Drinking

Beer District

CRAFT BEER

12 🍺 MAP P98, B3

One of Nice's coolest new nightspots, Beer District pours a regularly rotating line-up of 16 draught microbrews and 50 bottled beers from all over the world. The vibe is chilled and friendly, with free tastes cheerfully offered and little bowls of peanuts for snacking. (📞06 75 10 26 36; www.beerdistrict.fr; 13 rue Cassini; ⏰6pm-1am Tue-Sat; 🚊1 to Garibaldi, 2 to Port Lympia)

Rosalina Bar

BAR

13 🍺 MAP P98, C3

Way back before Le Port-Garibaldi became so trendy, Rosalina was the neighbourhood's nightlife pioneer. A decade later, it's still an

From Backwater to Bohemian Hotspot

Looking at this neighbourhood today, you'd never guess it was a swampy backwater until the 18th century. Unlike Marseille to the west and Genoa to the east, Nice never had a natural harbour suitable for large-scale commerce, so until the castle came toppling down in 1706 and Charles Emmanuel III commissioned the construction of Port Lympia in 1749, Nice was more important as a military stronghold than as a port.

Fast forward three centuries and everything's changed. The port is packed with passengers bound for Corsica, Cannes and Monaco, while the streets around place Garibaldi have become Nice's trendiest neighbourhood, buzzing with restaurants, shops and nightlife.

inviting, friendly spot for drinks or dinner, whether you're sipping wine and nibbling complimentary crostini with killer olive tapenade on the outdoor terrace, or downing a cocktail beside the piano and the swing in the whimsically decorated interior. (☏04 93 89 34 96; www.facebook.com/bar.rosalina; 16 rue Lascaris; ☺6.30pm-12.30am Mon-Sat; 🚋1 to Garibaldi, 2 to Port Lympia)

Rosé!
WINE BAR

15 🚋 MAP P98, C3

The concept is simple and the results agreeable at this recently opened wine bar. The extensive wine list skews heavily towards the top-quality rosés for which southern France is famous (though reds and whites are also available if you really *must*). Friends congregate for after-work aperitifs and late-afternoon snacks such as *barbajuans* (deep-fried ravioli stuffed with chard and cheese). (☏04 93 07 68 40; www.bar-rose.com; 22 rue François

Guisol; ☺6pm-midnight Tue-Sun; 🚋2 to Port Lympia)

Workhouse Café
CAFE

15 🚋 MAP P98, A2

Young freelancers are the focus at this recently opened 'coworking' space at the edge of place Garibaldi, but the general public is also welcome at the high-ceilinged on-site cafe. The coffee here is top-notch, as are the daily brunch offerings announced on the floor-to-ceiling chalkboard, from banana bread to veggie toast to scrambled eggs with smoked salmon or bacon. (☏04 93 01 27 25; www.workhousecafe.com; 64 blvd Risso; ☺8.30am-6.30pm Mon-Fri; 📶; 🚋1 to Garibaldi)

Comptoir Central Électrique
BAR

16 🚋 MAP P98, B2

Once a lighting factory (check out the light-bulb collection inside), now a hip-and-happening Port

Le Petit Marais

Parisians might scoff at the idea, but this district is lovingly nicknamed Le Petit Marais after the trendy Marais district in Paris. The compact tangle of streets wedged between place Garibaldi and Port Lympia buzz with happening eating, drinking and boutique shopping spots, firmly off the tourist radar but in the address book of every trendy local.

Dining options here range from humble eateries selling *socca* and *pissaladière* (onion tart) to bohemian vegan and tapas places, to top-end restaurants with impeccable gastronomic credentials. As for drinking, it's hard to walk for more than a minute without running into an intriguing bar or nightspot. Rue Bonaparte is the best street for bar-hopping, with plenty of other great options along rue Cassini, rue Lascaris and rue Bavastro. On the east side of the port, quai des Deux Emmanuels is another atmospheric spot for late-afternoon beers or aperitifs, with the setting sun casting a golden glow on the harbour's multihued facades.

Rue Bonaparte and surrounding side streets are home to a variety of quirky independent boutiques. The port area is also Nice's antiques hotspot, with dozens of shops and a monthly open-air *brocante* (flea market) filling place Garibaldi from 8am to 5pm on the third Saturday of every month.

Lympia bar with slouchy sofas, industrial-chic decor, and loads of beers and wines by the glass. There's a blackboard menu of snacks to share too. (📞06 77 52 02 08, 04 93 14 09 62; 10 rue Bonaparte; 🕐8am-12.30am Mon-Sat, from 5pm Sun; 🚊1 to Garibaldi)

Le Café des Chineurs BAR

17 🚇 MAP P98, B2

A young, hip crowd gravitates to this strategically placed bar at the corner of place Garibaldi and rue Bonaparte – the very epicentre of Petit Marais nightlife. It heaves from aperitif time into the wee hours, thanks to an international tapas menu (mainly focused on fried snacks, cheese and charcuterie) and a wide array of mixed drinks. (📞04 93 89 09 62; 1 rue Cassini; 🕐11am-midnight Mon-Sat; 🚊1 to Garibaldi)

L'Autre Part WINE BAR

18 🚇 MAP P98, C3

Organic and artisanal vintages rule the roost at this welcoming wine bar on lively rue Lascaris. Sip a glass or order a bottle from the well-stocked cellar, accompanied by snacks of cheese, charcuterie or delectable Cantabrian sardines.

(📞 09 81 10 91 01; www.lautrepart-nice.com; 10 rue Lascaris; 🕙 10am-2.30pm Mon-Fri, 5.30pm-12.30am Mon-Sat; 🚋 1 to Garibaldi, 2 to Port Lympia)

Entertainment

Cinéma Mercury   CINEMA

19 ⭐ MAP P98, B2

The neighbourhood's favourite cinema screens a good mix of current releases and independent films, including many in English. (📞 04 93 55 37 81; http://mercury. departement06.fr; 16 place Garibaldi; 🚋 1 to Garibaldi)

Shopping

Au Bonheur des Cocottes   VINTAGE

20 🔒 MAP P98, C2

Vintage clothing, jewellery, accessories and antique knick-knacks are just the beginning at this sweet boutique tucked among the bars and restaurants of rue Lascaris. You'll usually find the shop's energetic owners hard at work painting original artwork, sewing, embroidering,

fixing up and otherwise embellishing their latest finds. Want to join in? The store also offers a variety of arts-focused workshops. (📞 09 53 74 79 15; www.aubonheurdescocottes. com; 19 rue Lascaris; 🕙 10.30am-7.30pm Tue-Thu, to 9.30pm Fri & Sat; 🚋 1 to Garibaldi, 2 to Port Lympia)

Village Ségurane   ANTIQUES

21 🔒 MAP P98, B3

A must for antiques-lovers, this place gathers multiple dealers under a single roof in the heart of Nice's Port neighbourhood. (📞 04 93 26 95 05; 2 rue Antoine Gautier; 🕙 10am-noon & 3-6.30pm Mon-Sat; 🚋 1 to Garibaldi, 2 to Port Lympia)

Rodolphe Delcroix   MUSICAL INSTRUMENTS

22 🔒 MAP P98, C3

Down in the heart of Nice's antiques district, this amazing shop specialises in vintage musical instruments of every description, from hunting horns to Neapolitan mandolins. (📞 04 92 04 96 33; www. musicantic.eu; 15 rue Emmanuel Philibert; 🚋 1 to Garibaldi, 2 to Port Lympia)

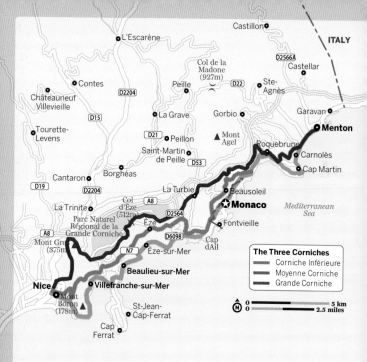

Worth a Trip 🚗
The Three Corniches

A compelling trio of corniches (coastal roads) hug the cliffs between Nice's port and Monaco, affording spectacular views of the Med. For the grandest vistas, it's the Grande Corniche you want, but the Moyenne Corniche runs a close scenic second. The lowest of all, the Corniche Inférieure, allows access to a string of snazzy coastal resorts.

Getting There

🚌 From Nice, Lignes d'Azur bus 116 to La Turbie; bus 82 to Èze; bus 81 to St-Jean-Cap-Ferrat.

🚌 From Nice to Villefranche-sur-Mer, Beaulieu-sur-Mer and Cap d'Ail on the Corniche Inférieure.

Grande Corniche

Views from the cliff-hanging Grande Corniche are mesmerising, and if you're driving, you'll probably want to stop at every bend to admire the unfolding vistas. Alfred Hitchcock was sufficiently impressed to use it as a backdrop for his film *To Catch a Thief* (1956), starring Cary Grant and Grace Kelly. Tragically, Kelly died in 1982 after crashing her car on this very same road. The most noteworthy village along the Grande Corniche is hilltop **La Turbie**, known for its imposing Roman triumphal monument.

Moyenne Corniche

Cut through rock in the 1920s, the Moyenne Corniche takes drivers from Nice past the **Col de Villefranche** (149m), **Èze** and **Beausoleil** (the French town bordering Monaco's Monte Carlo). Hikers can walk down from the gorgeous hilltop village of Èze to its coastal counterpart, **Èze-sur-Mer**, via the steep Sentier Nietzsche, a 45-minute footpath named after German philosopher Nietzsche, who started writing *Thus Spake Zarathustra* while staying in Èze (and enjoying this path).

Corniche Inférieure

Skimming the villa-lined waterfront between Nice and Monaco, the Corniche Inférieure, built in the 1860s, passes through the towns of Villefranche-sur-Mer, St-Jean-Cap-Ferrat, Beaulieu-sur-Mer, Èze-sur-Mer and Cap d'Ail. The views between Beaulieu-sur-Mer and Èze-sur-Mer are particularly dramatic, with sheer cliffs plunging directly into the sea. For more detailed inspiration, see our walking itineraries for **Beaulieu-sur-Mer** (p108) and **St-Jean-Cap-Ferrat** (p110).

★ Top Tips

o Don't miss La Turbie's amazing **Trophée des Alpes** (📞04 93 41 20 84; www.trophee-auguste. fr; 18 av Albert 1er; adult/child €6/free; ⏱9.30am-1pm & 2.30-6.30pm Tue-Sun mid-May–mid-Sep, 10am-1.30pm & 2.30-5pm rest of year). This columned monument, built in 6 BC to celebrate Emperor Augustus' victory over the Celto-Ligurian Alpine tribes, teeters on the highest point of the old Roman road.

o If walking the Sentier Nietzsche, take bus 82 up to Èze, hike down to Èze-sur-Mer, and ride the train back to Nice.

✗ Take a Break

o You'll find a few cafes and bistros en route, but consider packing a picnic for a spontaneous roadside lunch.

o Tempted to linger overnight? Èze's lavish **Château Eza** (📞04 93 41 12 24; www.chateaueza.com; rue de la Pise; d from €370; ❄🛜) is the place to splurge.

Walking Tour 🥾

Beaulieu's Backstreets & Beaches

Surrounded by stunning scenery, abounding in noble vestiges of belle-époque architecture and graced with one of Mediterranean France's mildest climates, the seaside village of Beaulieu-sur-Mer is an enchanting spot. Despite its obvious touristic appeal, Beaulieu has retained – more so than many Côte d'Azur resorts – a sense of history and local community that continue to stand the test of time.

Getting There

🚌 Lignes d'Azur bus 81 or 100 from Nice (20 minutes).

🚆 To Beaulieu-sur-Mer station (10 minutes from Nice Ville).

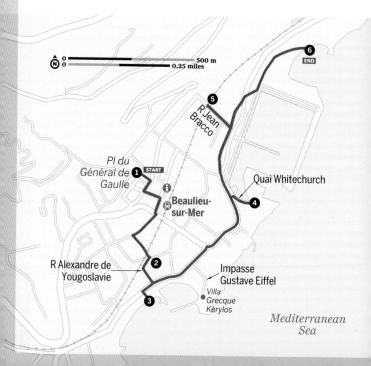

6 END

5

R Jean Bracco

Pl du Général de Gaulle 1 START

Beaulieu-sur-Mer

Quai Whitechurch

4

R Alexandre de Yougoslavie

2

Impasse Gustave Eiffel

3

Villa Grecque Kérylos

Mediterranean Sea

0 500 m
0 0.25 miles

❶ Marché de Beaulieu-sur-Mer

Beaulieu mornings kick off with a trip to the lively fruit and vegetable **market** (place du Général de Gaulle; ⏺8.30am-1pm). Mediterranean produce takes centre stage here, including locally grown citrus and olives. On July and August evenings, the belle-époque bandstand in the adjacent square forms the scenic backdrop for Beaulieu's series of summer concerts.

❷ Tennis Club de Beaulieu

The ping and whizz of tennis balls greets you at Beaulieu's venerable **tennis club** (☎04 93 01 05 19; www.itf-beaulieu.com; 4 rue Alexandre de Yougoslavie), founded In 1899 by British furniture magnate Sir Blundell Maple. The hard-packed red-clay courts have hosted everyone from kings to budding superstars – but everyday Berlugans (Beaulieu residents) are equally welcome. Pull up a plastic chair any time of day and watch club members compete.

❸ Plage des Fourmis

Perhaps no place better epitomises Beaulieu's timeless allure than this pretty **beach** at the centre of town. Backed by a palm-lined promenade and the city's century-old casino, it gazes across a sheltered bay towards the Villa Grecque Kérylos, a magnificent turn-of-the-20th-century faux-Greek villa. Families flock here for the calm waters and convenient in-town location.

❹ Port des Pêcheurs

Yachts and pleasure craft are the first thing you'll likely notice when you gaze out over Beaulieu's **port** (quai Whitechurch), hence the French name Port de Plaisance. But tucked away at the southern edge, a small coterie of fishermen still bring in their catch each morning. Come by at 9am or so to see them unloading directly onto the wharf.

❺ L'Olivaie

A visit to this **olive-shaded enclave** (rue Jean Bracco) on the edge of town feels like you're stepping back into another century, before casinos and easy rail access made the French Riviera famous. Locals relax on benches beneath ancient olive branches, reading or chatting with friends. It's also a perennial draw for kids, who come here for impromptu games of football.

❻ Plage Petite Afrique

'Little Africa' perfectly describes this hot and sunny stretch of sand. Dwarfed by the dramatic cliffs at Beaulieu's eastern edge, this long public **beach** is another long-standing family favourite. Umbrella pines create shade for little ones swinging and sliding in the playground, beach volleyball games spontaneously materialise, and swimmers dive from the platform just offshore.

Walking Tour 🥾

St-Jean-Cap-Ferrat

Ah, the fortunate few who call St-Jean-Cap-Ferrat home! Life on this gorgeous green peninsula 9km east of Nice remains close to nature and delightfully removed from the hectic pace of modern life. Some of France's most pristine coastal trails invite you to slow to a walking pace and appreciate the peninsula's uncommon beauty.

Getting There

🚌 Lignes d'Azur bus 81 from Promenade des Arts in Nice (35 minutes).

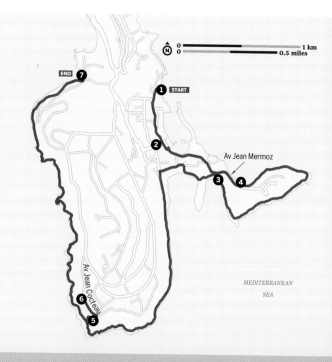

1 Plage Cros deï Pin

St-Jean's original public beach has been a local hotspot since the 1930s, when Somerset Maugham's former chef opened a community centre here. Families love the playground and beach volleyball, and everybody loves the **buvette** (snack bar; plage Cros deï Pin; sandwiches €4.50-5.90; 🕑7.30am-8.30pm May-Sep) run by local fixture Jean-Marc, where *pan bagnat*, coffee and beer are sold all day at nontourist prices.

2 La Civette

Sepia-toned pictures of St-Jean c 1930 show this cafe, already known as **La Civette** (📞04 93 76 04 14; 1 place Clemenceau; 🕑10am-7pm), on St-Jean's central square. Nearly a century later, it remains a popular local hang-out for coffee, wine and watching the world go by.

3 Jardin de la Paix

Shaded by fragrant pine trees and dotted with sculptures, this aptly named **peace park** is beloved as a quiet place to contemplate the sea before a walk along the 3km coastal loop that starts here. In summer a food truck sells snacks, and in August the whole town converges here for St-Jean's open-air jazz festival.

4 Plage Paloma

This idyllic crescent-shaped **cove** (av Jean Mermoz) is everyone's favourite summer getaway, with spellbinding views across to Beaulieu-sur-Mer and the cliffs of Èze. The private central beach here seduces tourists with its pricey restaurant, sunloungers and umbrellas – but savvy locals pack a picnic and flock to the free public sections on either side.

5 Phare du Cap-Ferrat

The classic St-Jean-Cap-Ferrat walk is the 7km Tour du Cap-Ferrat, which skirts the water's edge from St-Jean around the peninsula's wild outer reaches. Watch for residents walking their dogs out towards the **lighthouse** at Cap-Ferrat's southern tip.

6 Villa Santo Sospir

Unique among Cap Ferrat's many lavish villas is **Villa Santo Sospir** (📞04 93 76 00 16; www.villasanto-sospir.fr; 14 av Jean Cocteau; guided tour €12; 🕑by appointment only), where artist Jean Cocteau spent years adorning the walls with mythology-themed frescoes. It's open for occasional tours, concerts and public events.

7 Plage de Passable

Locals will tell you that sunset at **Plage de Passable** is among St-Jean-Cap-Ferrat's *incontournable* (not-to-be-missed) experiences. This beach on the peninsula's western edge gazes straight across at the ochre-hued villas of Villefranche-sur-Mer – never more splendid than when illuminated by late-afternoon sun.

Explore ⊚
Monaco

Squeezed into just 200 hectares, Monaco might be the world's second-smallest country, but what it lacks in size it makes up for in attitude. A riot of high-rise hotels, super yachts and apartment blocks stacked domino-like up steep hillsides, this tiny principality remains an eternal magnet for high-rollers, hedonists and the auto-racing fans who flock here for its annual Formula One Grand Prix.

Spend your morning touring the magnificent Casino de Monte Carlo (p114), then descend to the Marché de la Condamine (p137) for a reasonably priced lunch. Afterwards, head for historic Le Rocher, where you can visit the prince's palace (p126), the cathedral (p127) and the oceanographic museum (p118). If it's sunny, climb the hill to enjoy the remarkable vegetation and spectacular city views at Jardin Exotique (p126). Return downhill for ice cream at Pierre Geronimi (p129), waterfront drinks at Brasserie de Monaco (p132) or dinner at La Montgolfière (p129), followed by evening gambling at the casino.

Getting There & Around

Monaco's streets largely parallel the waterfront, interconnected by a pedestrian-friendly network of staircases, escalators and public lifts that help visitors avoid steep uphill walks.

🚆 Service every 20 minutes to Nice (€4.10, 25 minutes).

🚌 Lignes d'Azur (www.lignesdazur.com) runs bus 100 to Nice (€1.50, 45 minutes) every 15 minutes.

🚌 CAM (www.cam.mc) has six local lines, reaching anywhere in Monaco within 15 minutes.

Neighbourhood Map on p124

Monaco cityscape OSTILL/GETTY IMAGES ©

Top Sight 📷

Casino de Monte Carlo

The very emblem of Monaco and the cornerstone of the Riviera's glitzy allure, this belle-époque beauty revived the Grimaldi family's fortunes overnight when it opened in 1866 and still works its magic on all who venture near. Whether you're a seasoned gambler, a nostalgic James Bond fan or a curious onlooker, Monte Carlo's casino will make a lasting impression.

◉ **MAP P124, F3**

www.casinomontecarlo.com; place du Casino

morning visit incl audio-guide adult/child Oct-Apr €14/10, May-Sep €17/12, salons ordinaires gaming Oct-Apr €14, May-Sep €17

🕑 visits 9am-1pm, gaming 2pm-late

Atrium du Casino

The casino's grand atrium is paved in marble and lined with 28 Ionic columns, which support a balustrade gallery canopied with a Parisian engraved glass ceiling. This was the site of the original Monte Carlo casino, where gamblers were famously serenaded by a 15-piece orchestra. These days it's essentially a glorified 'lobby', the first room you pass through on your way to the actual casino. Exit to your left and enter the **Salon Renaissance**, which boasts a collection of antique and modern slot machines.

Salle Europe

The Salle Europe is the oldest part of the casino and its main gaming room. *Trente et quarante* and European roulette continue to be played here, as they have been since 1865. Enormous Bohemian glass chandeliers, each weighing 150kg, hang from an ornate circular glass ceiling supported by onyx columns banded with bronze. The bull's-eye windows around the room originally served as security observation points.

Salon Rose

After smoking was banned in the gaming rooms, the Salon Rose (Pink Room) was opened in 1903 as a gathering place for smokers. Nowadays it's a **restaurant**, open to the general public, and the only smokers you'll see are *Les Fumeuses,* the voluptuous cigarillo-smoking ladies painted on the ceiling by Italian artist Massimiliano Gallelli. Their gazes follow you as you walk around the room. A series of tall French doors offer tantalising glimpses of palm trees and the Mediterranean just outside.

Salle Blanche

A superb lounge, the 'White Room' is graced with an elegant mosaic-inlaid bar, backed by

★ Top Tips

o After 2pm when gaming begins, admission is strictly for 18 years and over; photo ID is obligatory.

o Don't wear trainers. A jacket for men is not obligatory but is recommended in the gaming rooms (and is compulsory in the evenings in the *salons privés*).

o In the main room (Salle Europe), the minimum bet is €5/10/20/25/40 for roulette/poker/ *trente et quarante/* blackjack/*punto banco*.

✕ Take a Break

Feast on Italian fare at Le Train Bleu (p130), the casino's recreation of a belle-époque railway dining car.

Snag a prime seat and people-watch from the casino-facing terrace at Café de Paris (p133).

a long wall of windows that open onto an outdoor gaming terrace with stunning Mediterranean views. The caryatids on the ceiling were modelled on fashionable courtesans such as La Belle Otéro, who placed her first bet here aged 18. On the far wall is a painting depicting La Belle Otéro and her companions Cléo de Mérode and Liane de Pougy as the Three Graces. This is one of the salons privés (p117), with tables for blackjack, Texas hold'em, English and European routette, and *punto banco* (baccarat).

Salles Touzet

Named for architect Jules Touzet and opened in 1890, this vast partitioned hall, 21m by 24m, is one of the casino's *salons privés*. It is decorated in lavish oak, Tonkin mahogany and oriental jasper panelling, which are offset by vast canvases, Marseille bronzes, Italian mosaics, sculptural reliefs and a 12m-high stained-glass ceiling. The gaming tables here feature blackjack and Texas hold'em poker.

Salle Médecin

Also known as Salle Empire because of its extravagant Empire-style decor, Monégasque architect François Médecin's gaming room was designed to accommodate the casino's biggest gamblers, and it remains one of the casino's more exclusive *salons privés,* with one part still hidden from prying eyes as a *super-privé* room. A popular filming location, it appears in the movies *Never Say Never Again* and *Golden Eye,* where James Bond him-

Salle Garnier (Opéra de Monte Carlo)

Salons Ordinaires, Salons Privés & Salons Super-Privés

The Casino de Monte Carlo is divided into *salons ordinaires* (ordinary rooms), *salons privés* (private rooms) and *salons super-privés* (the exclusive domain of serious gamblers).

Anyone (including children) can visit the *salons ordinaires* and *salons privés* on a self-guided audio tour during the morning hours when dress codes are relaxed and no gambling is taking place. After 2pm any adult who is suitably dressed is also welcome to gamble in the *salons ordinaires*, including the Salle Europe (gaming tables) and the Salles Renaissance and Amérique (slot machines only).

Access to the *salons privés* is limited; in 2018 the casino announced a new policy restricting *salons privés* to Gold and Platinum members of their 'frequent gambler' club. Meanwhile, the *salons super-privés* remain permanently off limits to all but the most extravagant high-rollers.

self can be seen striding across the room. The attached veranda has stunning views of the Bay of Roquebrune-Cap-Martin.

Salle Garnier

Also known as the Opéra de Monte Carlo (p135), the Salle Garnier is Monaco's opera house, hosting performances of opera, ballet and classical music throughout the year. Named for architect Charles Garnier, who also designed the Palais Garnier opera house in Paris, it directly adjoins the casino but has its own separate entrance and is not part of the casino tour. Taking eight months to build and two years to restore (2004–06), the opéra's original statuary was rehabilitated using original moulds saved by the creator's grandson. Individual air-con and heating vents are installed beneath each of the 525 seats.

Top Sight 📷
Musée Océanographique de Monaco

Housed in a dazzling Baroque Revival building built into an 85m cliff above the Mediterranean, Monaco's top museum is a stunner. Equally note-worthy for its audacious architecture, its superb collections and its unique history, the museum was the brainchild of Prince Albert I (1848–1922), a devoted marine scientist whose trips from the Mediterranean to the Arctic in the late 19th century yielded many new discoveries and a host of specimens.

◉ MAP P124, E5

📞 93 15 36 00

www.oceano.mc

av St-Martin

adult/child high season
€16/12, low season €11/7

🕙 9.30am-8pm Jul & Aug,
10am-7pm Apr-Jun & Sep,
to 6pm Oct-Mar

Aquarium

The museum's centrepiece is its aquarium – one of the oldest in Europe – with a 6m-deep lagoon where marine predators are separated from colourful tropical fish by a coral reef. Kids are mesmerised by the vertically partitioned, two-storey main tank, whose glass walls reveal sharks patrolling on one side while comically named small fry like the bluespine unicornfish and the blackspotted rubberlip swim merrily about on the other. In all, there are around 90 tanks in the aquarium containing a dazzling 450 Mediterranean and tropical species, sustained by 250,000L of freshly pumped seawater per day.

Discovering Oceanographic History

Upstairs, two huge colonnaded rooms retrace the history of oceanography and marine biology through photographs, specimens, vintage scuba gear and interactive displays, with a strong focus on Albert I's pioneering work and contributions to the field. Afterwards, climb to the panoramic rooftop terrace and cafe for dazzling views of Monaco and the Mediterranean.

Close Encounters with Marine Life

School holidays usher in feel-the-fish sessions in the kid-friendly **tactile basin**, where visitors can handle starfish, sea urchins and baby sharks. Hourly light shows are held in the **Salle de la Baleine**, with its 18m-long whale skeleton suspended in mid-air. A new outdoor turtle tank, set to open in 2019, will allow the public to observe injured marine turtles rehabilitated by the museum's marine biologists.

★ **Top Tips**

The rooftop terrace and cafe boast sweeping views of the principality and the Med.

Save a few cents by buying a combined ticket covering same-day admission to both the Palais Princier (p126) and the Musée Océanographique; both sights sell it.

✗ **Take a Break**

Indulge in a coffee, tea or hot chocolate break at Chocolaterie de Monaco (p132).

Stroll five minutes to U Cavagnetu (p130) for reasonably priced Monégasque lunch specials.

Walking Tour 🚶

Monte Carlo Casino to Monaco Ville

Monaco's most iconic sights trace a graceful arc around the contours of La Condamine harbour. This leisurely hour-long stroll takes you from the belle-époque splendour of Monte Carlo's casino to the clifftop core of the medieval city, offering sublime sea and garden perspectives en route.

Walk Facts

Start Casino de Monte Carlo

End Musée Océanographique

Length 2km; one hour

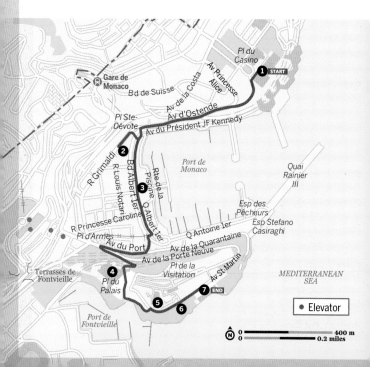

❶ From the Casino to the Port

Starting in front of Monte Carlo's legendary **casino** (p114), walk towards Monaco's steeply perched medieval old town, Le Rocher, which beckons from a hilltop across the water. As you make a curving descent to the port of La Condamine, you're tracing the route of Monaco's iconic Formula One Grand Prix.

❷ Grand Prix Gear

If Grand Prix swag tickles your fancy, cross bd Albert 1er upon arrival at the waterfront to reach **La Boutique** (p136). This official shop of Monaco's automobile club can sell you everything from model cars to racing jackets.

❸ Swimming & Skating

Back on the waterfront, watch crowds frolic at **Stade Nautique Rainier III** (p128), home to an Olympic-sized pool in summer and an ice-skating rink in winter.

❹ Changing of the Guard

At the port's far end, follow signs for the Palais Princier and climb the zigzag Rampe Majeur into Le Rocher. If you time things right, you'll reach Place du Palais, the square in front of the **prince's palace** (p126), in time to see the 11.55am changing of the guard. The knee-sock-wearing crew hasn't had to do much actual defending of the principality in recent memory, but their daily drum-beating spectacle is still good fun.

❺ Paying Respects to the Princess

Next, follow the signposted clifftop path towards **Cathédrale de Monaco** (p127), where you can pay your respects to Grace Kelly, the movie-star-turned princess who died tragically in a 1982 car accident. Her tomb in the cathedral's apse is often covered in fresh flowers placed by the queues of admirers.

❻ Cliffside Gardens

Enjoy spellbinding views of Monaco's Fontvieille harbour as you enter the gorgeous **Jardins St-Martin** (p127), draped in greenery and adorned with statues and fountains. From up here, it's easy to perceive the principality's dual strategy for growth: build up (skyscrapers) and out (landfill). The latter technique has increased Monaco's 'land' area by 25%.

❼ Oceanographic Museum

At the far end of the park is the extraordinary **Musée Océanographique de Monaco** (p118), which soars straight out of the cliff face and towers over the Mediterranean. After lunch in the old town, Le Rocher, return to spend the rest of the afternoon exploring the fine aquarium and historic collection of marine artefacts inside.

Walking Tour 🥾

Monaco's Hidden Local Havens

Monaco's 8000 ancestral Monégasque citizens
are easily outnumbered by 29,000 adoptive residents from 139 other countries, 45,000 French
and Italian guest workers, and the never-ending
flood of foreign tourists. Yet even with this crush of
outsiders, the principality's locals still have some
special havens that they can call their own.

Walk Facts

Start Parc Princesse
Antoinette

End Crique Ciappaira

Length 2km; one hour

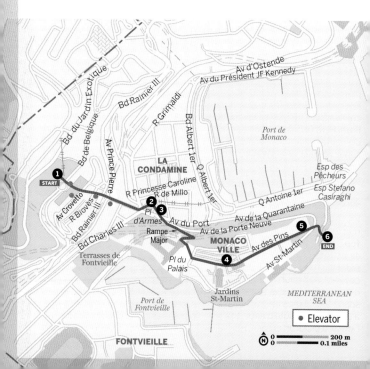

❶ Parc Princesse Antoinette

Despite Monaco's rampant high-rise development, Monégasques are big nature-lovers. Jogging and picking wild mushrooms remain favourite pastimes, and 25% of the country is still conserved as green space, including this hidden hillside **park** (🕑8.30am-6pm) below the Jardin Exotique. School kids hunt for eggs here every Easter, and the adjoining school raises chickens and vegetables among the ancient olive trees.

❷ Marché de la Condamine

This fresh produce **market** (p137) fills place d'Armes every morning throughout the year. Families do their regular shopping here, while kids frolic on the adjacent playground. Thanks to the Riviera's climate, lemons and oranges are available here in midwinter. From Parc Princesse Antoinette, descend to place d'Armes via a series of staircases and elevators, following signs for Avs Crovetto and Prince Pierre.

❸ Chez Roger

Shoppers typically save their morning break for this beloved **food stall** (📞93 50 80 20; Marché de la Condamine, 15 place d'Armes; socca €3; 🕑10am-3pm) in the covered food court just off place d'Armes. The speciality here is *socca*, a chickpea pancake that's a staple of the Côte d'Azur diet. Demand picks up around 10am.

❹ Chapelle de la Miséricorde

Catholicism remains Monaco's state religion, with some 90% of citizens identifying as Catholic. While visitors regularly make pilgrimages to the 19th-century Cathédrale de Monaco to see the tomb of Princess Grace, this smaller, earlier **chapel** (place de la Mairie) is where many locals come to celebrate the Latin Mass held here at 6pm each Sunday and to admire the 17th-century paintings.

❺ Club Bouliste du Rocher

Much as in neighbouring France and Italy, *pétanque* is a favourite pastime in Monaco. This unassuming-looking **club** (www.centreformation-cbr.com; av des Pins), marked by a simple red sign, made the French national semifinals in 2018. Glance through the gate and you'll see members eating lunch in the canteen at the back, then hitting the pitch to toss boules later in the afternoon.

❻ Crique Ciappaira

Tucked away below the cliffs on the south side of Le Rocher is this secret shingle **beach** (Plage des Pêcheurs), known mostly to resident Monégasques. Old stone steps career steeply down to the water, where there's just enough space to lay a towel. When the sun's shining, you'll find locals here even in the dead of winter. In stormy weather, it becomes utterly impassable.

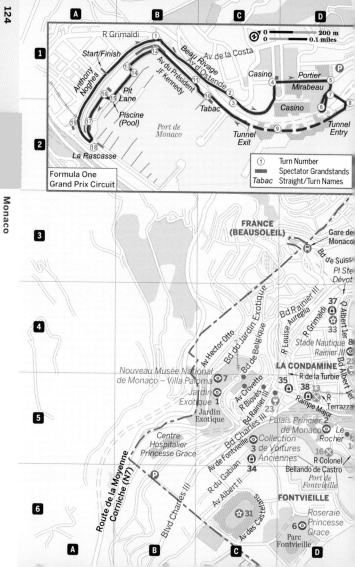

A B C D

R Grimaldi

Start/Finish

Anthony Noghes

Beau Rivage
Av d'Ostende

Av de la Costa

Casino

Portier

Mirabeau

Casino

Av du Président
JF Kennedy

Pit Lane

Piscine
(Pool)

Port de
Monaco

Tabac

Tunnel
Exit

Tunnel
Entry

La Rascasse

Formula One
Grand Prix Circuit

200 m
0.1 miles

① Turn Number
Spectator Grandstands
Tabac Straight/Turn Names

FRANCE
(BEAUSOLEIL)

Gare de
Monaco

Bd de Suisse

Pl Ste
Dévot

Bd Rainier III

R Grimaldi

Av Louise Aureglia

O Albert 1er

Stade Nautique
Rainier III

37

33

8

Bd Albert 1er

Av Hector Otto

Bd du Jardin Exotique

Bd de Belgique

LA CONDAMINE

R de la Turbie

Nouveau Musée National
de Monaco – Villa Paloma

7

Av Crovetto

R Biovès

Bd Rainier III

35

38

13

Jardin
Exotique 1

Rampe Major

R
Terrazza

Jardin
Exotique

23

Palais Princier
de Monaco

2

Le
Rocher

Centre
Hospitalier
Princesse Grace

Bd Charles III

Collection
de Voitures
Anciennes

3

16

R Colonel

Bellando de Castro

Av de Fontvieille

34

Port de
Fontvieille

R du Gabian

FONTVIEILLE

Roseraie
Princesse
Grace

Route de la Moyenne
Corniche (N7)

Blvd Charles III

Av Albert II

31

Av des Castelans

6

Parc
Fontvieille

Monaco

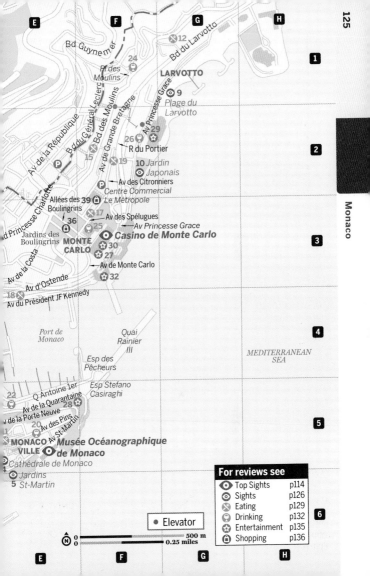

E
Bd Guynemer

F
24
Pl des
Moulins

⊗12
Bd du Larvotto

G

H

1

LARVOTTO

⊙9
Plage du
Larvotto

Av de la République

Bd du Général Leclerc

Bd des Moulins

Bd du Grande Bretagne

Av Princesse Grace

26
29
R du Portier

15
⊗19

10 Jardin
⊙ Japonais

2

Av de la Costa

Av de Princesse Charlotte

P

Av des Citronniers
Centre Commercial

Allées des 39 ⓐ Le Métropole
Boulingrins

36
⊗17
25 Av des Spélugues
Av Princesse Grace

⊙ Casino de Monte Carlo

MONTE
CARLO

30
27
Av de Monte Carlo

Jardins des
Boulingrins

32

3

Av de la Costa

Av d'Ostende
18⊗
Av du Président JF Kennedy

*Port de
Monaco*

*Quai
Rainier
III*

*MEDITERRANEAN
SEA*

4

*Esp des
Pêcheurs*

22
Q Antoine 1er
Av de la Quarantaine 28
Av de la Porte Neuve
20 Av des Pins
Av St-Martin

*Esp Stefano
Casiraghi*

5

⊗ MONACO Av
VILLE ⊙ *Musée Océanographique
de Monaco*

Cathédrale de Monaco
⊙ *Jardins
5 St-Martin*

6

• Elevator

N 0 — 500 m
0 — 0.25 miles

E   **F**   **G**   **H**

Monaco's Old Town

Monaco Ville, also called **Le Rocher**, is the only part of Monaco to have retained its original old town, complete with small, windy medieval lanes. The old town thrusts skywards on a pistol-shaped rock, its strategic location overlooking the sea that became the stronghold of the Grimaldi dynasty. There are various staircases up to Le Rocher; the best route up is via Rampe Major, which starts from place d'Armes near the port.

On your way up, look out for the statue of the late Prince Rainier looking down on his beloved Monaco, created by Dutch artist Kees Verkade in 2013.

Sights

Jardin Exotique

GARDENS

1 ◉ MAP P124, C5

Home to the world's largest succulent and cactus collection, from small echinocereus to 10m-tall African candelabras, the gardens tumble down the slopes of Moneghetti through a maze of paths, stairs and bridges. Views of the principality are spectacular. Admission includes the **Musée d'Anthropologie**, which displays prehistoric remains unearthed in Monaco, and a 35-minute guided tour of the **Grotte de l'Observatoire**. The prehistoric, stalactite- and stalagmite-laced cave is the only one in Europe where the temperature rises as you descend.

Bus 2 links Jardin Exotique with the town centre. (☎93 15 29 80; www.jardin-exotique.mc; 62 bd du Jardin Exotique; adult/child €7.20/3.80; ☉9am-7pm mid-May–mid-Sep, to 6pm rest of year)

Palais Princier de Monaco

PALACE

2 ◉ MAP P124, D5

Built as a fortress atop Le Rocher in the 13th century, this palace is the private residence of the Grimaldi family. It is protected by the blue-helmeted, white-socked Carabiniers du Prince; changing of the guard takes place daily at 11.55am, when crowds gather outside the gates to watch.Most of the palace is off limits, but you can get a glimpse of royal life on a tour of the glittering **state apartments**, where you can see some of the lavish furniture and priceless artworks collected by the family over the centuries. It's a good idea to buy tickets online in advance to avoid queuing. (☎93 25 18 31; www.palais.mc; place du Palais; adult/child €8/4, incl Collection de Voitures Anciennes car museum €11.50/5, incl Musée Océanographique €19/11; ☉10am-6pm Apr-Jun & Sep–mid-Oct, to 7pm Jul & Aug)

Collection de Voitures Anciennes

MUSEUM

3 ◉ MAP P124, C5

Starting in the early 1950s, car-mad Prince Rainier amassed an impressive array of over 100 classic automobiles, which he opened to the public in 1993. His haul includes various Ferraris, Maseratis, Lamborghinis, Rolls-Royces and several F1 and rally cars. The museum itself is basically an exhibition hall, but will move to its new purpose-built home by the harbour when it's completed in 2020. (Monaco Top Cars Collection; ☎92 05 28 56; www.mtcc.mc; Terrasses de Fontvieille; adult/child €6.50/3, incl Palais Princier de Monaco €11.50/5; ☾10am-6pm)

Cathédrale de Monaco

CATHEDRAL

4 ◉ MAP P124, E5

An adoring crowd continually shuffles past Prince Rainier's and Princess Grace's flower-adorned graves, located inside the cathedral choir of Monaco's 1875 Romanesque-Byzantine cathedral. (4 rue Colonel Bellando de Castro; admission free; ☾8.30am-6.45pm)

Jardins St-Martin

GARDENS

5 ◉ MAP P124, E6

The steep-sided, statue-studded Jardins St-Martin runs round the coast outside the Musée Océanographique. (admission free; ☾9am-sunset)

Cathédrale de Monaco

Stade Nautique Rainier III

Roseraie Princesse Grace

GARDENS

6 ◉ MAP P124, D6

Thoroughly revamped in 2014, this exuberant collection of over 4000 rose bushes – along with the adjacent Parc Fontvieille – stands out in dramatic contrast to the otherwise sterile high-rise environment of Fontvieille. The garden bursts with colour in springtime, with multihued roses climbing up arbours and encircling the trunks and branches of olive trees. (av des Papalins; admission free; P)

Nouveau Musée National de Monaco – Villa Paloma

GALLERY

7 ◉ MAP P124, C5

This pearly-white villa, built for an American in 1913 on a hillside near the Jardin Exotique, is part of Nouveau Musée National de Monaco, along with **Villa Sauber** (☎98 98 91 26; www.nmnm.mc; 17 av Princesse Grace; adult/child €6/free including Villa Paloma, free admission Sun; ☉10am-6pm). It hosts seasonal contemporary art exhibitions with an environmental theme (oceans, apocalypse etc). Also sells a combo ticket (€10) which includes entry to the Jardin Exotique (p126). (☎98 98 48 60; www.nmnm.mc; 56 bd du Jardin Exotique; adult/child €6/free incl Villa Sauber, free admission Sun; ☉10am-6pm)

Stade Nautique Rainier III

SWIMMING, ICE SKATING

8 ◉ MAP P124, D4

Smack in the middle of Monaco's port area, this Olympic-sized outdoor seawater pool has diving boards and a curly water slide. In winter it becomes an ice rink. (☏93 30 64 83; quai Albert 1er; morning/afternoon/evening/full day €3.20/4/2.40/5.70; ☖9am-8pm Jun-Aug, to 6pm Sep–mid-Oct & May, to 6pm Mon year-round)

Plage du Larvotto — SWIMMING

9 ◉ MAP P124, G1

At Monaco's eastern edge, this sandy crescent – dotted with beach chairs and umbrellas, crisscrossed with volleyball nets and backed by a palm-fringed boardwalk – is a favourite summer hang-out.

Jardin Japonais — GARDENS

10 ◉ MAP P124, F2

Sandwiched between built-up Monte Carlo, Larvotto and the Mediterranean, the Jardin Japonais is intended as a piece of paradise. It was blessed by a Shinto high priest, and quiet contemplation and meditation is encouraged. (Japanese Garden; av Princesse Grace; admission free; ☖9am-6.45pm Apr-Oct, to 5.45pm Nov-Mar)

Eating

La Montgolfière — FUSION €€€

11 ✕ MAP P124, E5

Monégasque chef Henri Geraci has worked in some of the Riviera's top restaurants, but he's now happily settled at his own establishment down a shady alleyway near the palace. Escoffier-trained, he's faithful to the French classics, but his travels have inspired a fondness for Asian flavours, so expect some exotic twists. The restaurant's small and sought after, so reserve ahead. (☏97 98 61 59; www.lamontgolfiere.mc; 16 rue Basse; 3-/4-course menu €47/54; ☖noon-2pm & 7.30-9.30pm Mon, Tue & Thu-Sat)

Pierre Geronimi — ICE CREAM

12 ✕ MAP P124, G1

A bit of a local's secret: Monaco's best ice creams and sorbets, made by its eponymous Corsican *maître glacier*. The flavours are exciting – try chestnut flour, beetroot, matcha tea or honey and pine nut – and for the ultimate indulgence, ask for it to be served cocktail-style in a glass *verrine*. He also creates delicious ice-cream cakes and patisseries. Don't say we didn't warn you. (☏97 98 69 11; www.glacespierregeronimi.com; 36 bd d'Italie; 1/2/3 scoops €3.80/6/8; ☖8am-7pm Mon-Sat Oct-Apr, 7.30am-7.30pm Mon-Sat & 10am-6pm Sun May-Sep)

Maison des Pâtes — ITALIAN €

13 ✕ MAP P124, D5

In the morning, locals besiege this stand in Marché de la Condamine (p130) for fresh pasta to take home; come lunchtime, it morphs into an informal restaurant, with more than a dozen pastas and a dozen sauces on offer at bargain prices. Choose your combo and chow done at one of the informal communal tables. (☏93 50 95 77;

Cheap Eats in Monaco

For tasty, excellent-value fare around shared tables, hit Monaco's fabulous food court, **Marché de la Condamine** (Map 124, D5; www.facebook.com/marche.condamine; 15 place d'Armes; ⏰7am-3pm Mon-Sat, to 2pm Sun), which is tucked beneath the arches behind the open-air place d'Armes market. Rock-bottom budget faves include fresh pasta from Maison des Pâtes and traditional Niçois *socca* from Chez Roger; there's also pizza and seafood from Le Comptoir, truffle cuisine from Truffle Bistrot, a deli, a cafe, a cheesemonger and more.

Marché de la Condamine, 15 place d'Armes; pasta €6.40-12; ⏰7am-3.30pm)

U Cavagnetu

MEDITERRANEAN €€

14 ⓧ MAP P124, D5

The crush of tourist-oriented restaurants in the narrow streets of Le Rocher may make you want to run screaming, but U Cavagnetu is worth sticking around for. The tasty line-up of authentic Monégasque treats includes *barbajuans* (deep-fried ravioli), *beignets de courgettes* (zucchini fritters) and *poulpe à la monégasque* (octopus stewed with tomatoes, onion, garlic, parsley and wine). (☎97 98 20 40; www.facebook.com/cavagnetu.monaco; 14 rue Comte Félix Gastaldi; plat du jour €16.50, menu €27.50; ⏰11am-10pm)

Le Train Bleu

ITALIAN €€€

For one of Monaco's most atmospheric dining experiences, head for Le Train Blue (see 30 ⓧ Map p124, F3) in the Casino de Monte Carlo. The menu is high-end Italian, served in a replica vintage belle-époque train car. (☎98 06 24 24; http://fr.montecarlosbm.com/restaurant-monaco; place du Casino; mains €25-68; ⏰2pm-5am)

Le Loga

INTERNATIONAL €€

15 ⓧ MAP P124, F2

On the main drag above the casino, Loga really shines on weekdays, when its wine-inclusive lunch *menus* are among the best deals in Monaco. Specialities include steaks, meal-sized salads and exquisite homemade gnocchi, along with other Italian fare. (☎93 30 87 72; www.loga.mc; 25 bd des Moulins; lunch menus €15-22, dinner menu €38, mains €16-42; ⏰8am-11pm Mon, Tue & Thu-Sat, 8am-7pm Wed)

Castel Roc

FRENCH €€€

16 ⓧ MAP P124, D5

This fine-dining stalwart has perhaps the most princely location in all of Monaco – it's literally steps from the palace's main gates, with a suntrap patio to boot. Well-heeled patrons come here for rich, traditional French food like stuffed rabbit saddle and slow-cooked lamb, served on sparkly china plates and starchy white tablecloths. The lunch *menu* is surprisingly good value. (📞93 30 36 68; www.castelrocmonaco.com; 1 place du Palais; 2-/3-course lunch menu €24/32, 3-/4-course dinner menu €48/59; 🕐12.30-2pm & 7.30-9.30pm Tue-Sun)

Tip Top INTERNATIONAL €€

17 🍴 MAP P124, F3

A favourite haunt of Monaco's night owls, this tiny, check-clothed bistro sticks out like a sore thumb, just a stone's throw from the fancy Café de Paris and the casino. It's been going for donkey's years and still draws in a loyal local crowd for its reliable, no-fuss pizzas and pastas, and its daily *plat du jour*. (📞93 50 69 13; www.facebook.com/TipTop-Monaco; 11 av des Spélugues; pizza €15-20, mains €16-38; 🕐9am-5am Mon-Sat, 6.15pm-midnight Sun; 📶)

La Marée SEAFOOD €€€

18 🍴 MAP P124, E4

La Marée's 'fish & chic' tagline says it all: if you're after seafood with a stunning sea view, then this swish rooftop restaurant at the Hotel Port-Plage is the place. From turbot, red mullet, sea bass and monkfish to seafood platters loaded with lobster and crustaceans, pescatarians will be properly pampered here. Monaco's jet-set turn out in force for Sunday brunch. (📞377 97 97 80 00; www.lamaree.mc; 7 av du Président JF Kennedy; mains €22-82; 🕐noon-11pm Mon-Fri, noon-midnight Sat & Sun)

U Cavagnetu restaurant

Serene Strolling on the Waterfront

A serene alternative to the sweaty hike with the crowds up Rampe Majeur to Le Rocher is a panoramic stroll along **Digue de Monaco**, the world's largest floating dyke, 28m wide and 352m long. Scale the steps at the end of quai Antoine 1er and bear left to the viewpoint at the dyke's far end, next to the cruise-ship terminal, for an outstanding Monte Carlo panorama.

Backtrack to Esplanade Stefano Casiraghi for a quick flop in the sun on the contemporary sun deck here; ladders allow you to dip into the water. Then weave your way along the coastal path and up through the shady Jardins St-Martin to Le Rocher. Look out for stone steps leading down to a secret shingle beach only locals know about.

Ristorante Mozza   ITALIAN €€

19 ⊗ MAP P124, F2

As its name suggests, Mozza's speciality is its eponymous cheese – directly imported from Italy, with multiple varieties to taste at the mozzarella bar. Otherwise, it's fine traditional Italian fare: sophisticated pizza and pastas, antipasti and (rather curiously) hamburgers. (☏97 77 03 04; www.mozza.mc; 11 rue du Portier; lunch menus €19-24, pizzas €14-24, mains €18-39; ⊗noon-2.30pm & 7.30-10.30pm Mon-Thu, to 11.30pm Fri-Sun; 🖉)

Drinking

Chocolaterie de Monaco   CAFE

20 ⊗ MAP P124, E5

For a sweet pick-me-up between the Palais Princier and the Musée Océanographique, this chocolate shop with attached cafe couldn't be better placed. Various drinks are on the menu, but hot chocolate (€5.20 to €5.90) is naturally the star. (☏97 97 88 88; www.chocolateriedemonaco.com; place de la Visitation; ⊗9.30am-6.30pm Mon-Sat, 10am-noon & 12.30-5.30pm Sun)

Brasserie de Monaco

MICROBREWERY

21 ⊗ MAP P124, D4

This bar down by La Condamine is Monaco's only microbrewery, and its organic lagers and ales pack the punters in. Inside it's all chrome, steel and big-screen TVs, and live sport and DJs keep the weekends extra busy. For a more chilled experience, head for the portside patio out the front. Happy hour's from 6pm to 8pm. (☏97 98 51 20; www.facebook.com/brasseriedemonacomc; 36 rte de la Piscine; ⊗noon-2am)

Rascasse

BAR

22 MAP P124, E5

This two-storey lounge bar down by the port draws the crowds at aperitif time, then morphs into Monaco's liveliest nightspot, with live music Monday through Friday and all-night DJs on weekends. (98 06 16 16; www.larascassemontecarlo.com; 1 quai Antoine; 4pm-5am)

Snowflake

CAFE

23 MAP P124, C5

Stop in for a spot of tea at this serene and stylish English bookshop, cafe, teahouse and work space. Decor is Scandinavian design, with armchairs to flop in as well as laptop-friendly desks. Check its Facebook page for creative workshops, readings and cultural happenings. (377 97 77 24 67; www.facebook.com/Snowflake Monaco; 1 Promenade Honoré II; 10am-7pm Mon-Fri)

Le Teashop

TEAROOM

24 MAP P124, F1

This super-stylish tea bar is all the rage with Monaco's ladies who lunch. There are more than 130 loose-leaf teas to choose from, served in a china pot, as a frothy latte or Asian-style with bubbles. The cakes are too good to resist. (97 77 47 47; www.leteashop.com; place des Moulins; 9am-7pm Mon-Sat)

Café de Paris

CAFE

25 MAP P124, F3

The *grande dame* of Monaco's cafes (founded in 1882), it's

Café de Paris

The Formula One Grand Prix

If there's one trophy a Formula One driver would like to have on the mantelpiece, it would have to be from the most glamorous race of the season, the Monaco Grand Prix. This race has everything. Its spectators are the most sensational: the merely wealthy survey the spectacle from Hôtel Hermitage, the really rich watch from their luxury yachts moored in the harbour, while the Grimaldis see the start and finish from the royal box at the port. Then there's the setting: the cars scream around the very centre of the city, racing uphill from the start/finish line to place du Casino, then downhill around a tight hairpin and two sharp rights to hurtle through a tunnel and run along the harbourside to a chicane and more tight corners before the start/finish.

But despite its reputation, the Monaco Grand Prix is not really one of the great races. The track is too tight and winding for modern Formula One cars, and overtaking is virtually impossible. The Brazilian triple world champion Nelson Piquet famously described racing at Monaco as like 'riding a bicycle around your living room'. Piquet clearly rides a much faster bicycle than most of us; Monaco may be the slowest race on the calendar, but the lap record is still over 160km/h, and at the fastest point on the circuit, cars reach 280km/h. Even the corner in the gloom of the tunnel is taken at 250km/h.

The 78-lap race happens on a Sunday afternoon in late May, the conclusion of several days of practice, qualifying and supporting races. Tickets (€30 to €1400) are theoretically available from the Automobile Club de Monaco online (www.acm.mc) or in Monaco at its billetterie (p136), but in practice the best seats sell out months in advance.

If you can't make the big event but are still eager to see car racing on the streets of Monaco, come in mid-May for the biannual **Grand Prix Historique de Monaco** (www.monacograndprixticket.com/grand-prix-historique; ☺May), featuring vintage racing cars.

perfect for *un petit café* and a spot of people-watching. Everything is chronically overpriced, and the waiters can be horrendously snooty, but it's the price you pay for a front-row view of Monte Carlo's razzamatazz. (☎98 06 76 23; www.facebook.com/cafede parismontecarlo; place du Casino; ☺8am-2am)

Sass Café
BAR

26 🟢 MAP P124, F2

A see-and-be-seen hang-out for Monaco's high-rollers, this perpetually packed piano bar is reminiscent of old-school cabarets with its shiny bar counter, lacquered grand piano (live music every night) and padded red walls. DJs keep things heaving into the wee hours. (🗐 93 25 52 00; www.sasscafe.com; 11 av Princesse Grace; ⏱8pm-4am)

Entertainment

Opéra de Monte Carlo
OPERA

27 ⭐ MAP P124, F3

Also known as the Salle Garnier, Monaco's opera house is an 1892 confection of neoclassical splendour adjoining Monte Carlo Casino, designed by Charles Garnier (who also designed the Paris opera house). The season runs from October through April. It also serves as a venue for concerts by the Monte Carlo Philharmonic Orchestra (www.opmc.mc) and dance performances by Les Ballets de Monte Carlo (www. balletsdemontecarlo.com). (Salle Garnier; 🗐ticket office 98 06 28 28; www.opera.mc; Casino de Monte Carlo, place du Casino)

Monaco Open-Air Cinema
CINEMA

28 ⭐ MAP P124, E5

Watch crowd-pleasing blockbusters, mostly in English, beneath the stars at the world's only 3D open-air cinema. Films start at 10pm nightly in June and July, and at 9.30pm in August and September. There are 500 seats but no advance reservations, so arrive when the doors open at 8.45pm (8.30pm August and September). (🗐93 25 86 80; www.cinemas2monaco.com; av de la Quarantaine; adult/child €12/9; ⏱mid-Jun–mid-Sep)

Grimaldi Forum
LIVE PERFORMANCE

29 ⭐ MAP P124, F2

This large auditorium hosts expos, trade shows, concerts by the Monte Carlo Philharmonic Orchestra (www.opmc.mc), dance performances by Les Ballets de Monte Carlo (www.balletsdemontecarlo.com) and more. (🗐ticket office 99 99 30 00; www.grimaldiforum.mc; 10 av Princesse Grace; ⏱noon-7pm Tue-Sat)

Atrium du Casino
BOOKING SERVICE

30 ⭐ MAP P124, F3

Tickets for events and spectacles. (🗐98 06 28 28; Casino de Monte Carlo, place du Casino; ⏱10am-5.30pm Tue-Sat)

Stade Louis II
SPECTATOR SPORT

31 ⭐ MAP P124, C6

The stadium is home to the AS Monaco football team. Buy match tickets from the ticket office inside or view the stadium as part of a 20-minute guided tour; just turn up at the respective time and buy a ticket. (🗐92 05 40 21;

ROSTISLAV GLINSKY/SHUTTERSTOCK ©

Le Métropole shopping centre

www.stadelouis2.mc; 7 av des Castelans; guided tour adult/child €5.20/2.60; ⏰tours 10.30am, 11.30am, 2.30pm, 3.30pm, 4.30pm Mon-Fri Apr-Sep)

Auditorium Rainier III

CLASSICAL MUSIC

32 ⭐ MAP P124, F3

Well regarded for its acoustics, this auditorium is the main venue for classical music concerts by the Monte Carlo Philharmonic Orchestra. (📞93 10 85 00; bd Louis II)

Automobile Club de Monaco

BOOKING SERVICE

33 ⭐ MAP P124, D4

Sells tickets for Monaco's F1 Grand Prix and other motoring events. (ACM; 📞93 15 26 00; www.acm.mc; 23 bd Albert 1er)

Shopping

Office des Émissions de Timbres-Poste

GIFTS & SOUVENIRS

34 🔒 MAP P124, C5

Collectors – and anyone else smitten with the quirky allure of stamps issued in the world's second-smallest country – should stop in at this official government office, which sells a wide variety of Monaco stamps, both past and present. (📞98 98 41 41; www. oetp-monaco.com; 23 av Albert II; ⏰9am-5pm Mon-Fri)

L'Orangerie

DRINKS

35 🔒 MAP P124, D5

The brainchild of expatriate Dubliner Philip Culazzo, l'Orangerie is an artisanal liqueur made with bitter oranges harvested from the citrus trees lining some of Monaco's streets. Grab a taste and bring home a bottle from this cute-as-a-button, bright orange boutique. (☑99 90 43 38; www.orangerie.mc; 9 rue de la Turbie; ☺9.30am-12.30pm & 2.30-5.30pm Mon-Fri)

Les Pavillons de Monte Carlo
MALL

36 🔒 MAP P124, E3

No, the Tellytubbies haven't moved into Monte Carlo. The five giant snow-white 'pebbles' that sprang up on the lawns of **Jardins des Boulingrins** in 2014 are a temporary home to the luxury boutiques previously housed in the now-demolished **Sporting d'Hiver**. Sometime in 2019, they'll all relocate to the spiffy new **Monaco 1** building, just downhill on place du Casino's southwest corner.

Among the high-end boutiques you'll find here are Chanel, McQueen, Sonia Rykiel and Dior. (allées des Boulingrins, place du Casino)

La Boutique de l'Automobile Club de Monaco
GIFTS & SOUVENIRS

37 🔒 MAP P124, D4

At this boutique run by Monaco's automobile club, you can buy the official T-shirt, along with zillions of other Monaco Grand Prix–themed accessories: shirts, bags, jeans, watches, model cars, noise-cancelling headphones, baby clothes... You get the idea. (☑97 70 45 35; www.monaco-grandprix.com; 46 rue Grimaldi; ☺9.30am-7pm Mon-Fri, from 10.30am Sat)

Marché de la Condamine
FOOD

38 🔒 MAP P124, D5

This open-air fruit and vegetable market, open daily year-round, is one of Monaco's most authentically local experiences – even if the prices are just as inflated as elsewhere in the principality. (www.facebook.com/marche. condamine; place d'Armes; ☺5.30am-12.30pm)

Le Métropole
MALL

39 🔒 MAP P124, F3

This shopping centre is probably the best place in Monaco to find more mainstream (read affordable) fashion and other goods. (☑93 50 15 36; www. metropoleshoppingmontecarlo.com; 17 av des Spélugues; ☺10am-7.30pm Mon-Sat)

Survival Guide

Place Garibaldi (p99) KIEV.VICTOR/SHUTTERSTOCK ©

Before You Go

Book Your Stay

o Accommodation in Nice is excellent and caters to all budgets, unlike many cities on the Côte d'Azur.

o Hotels charge substantially more in the Monaco Grand Prix in May.

o Book well in advance in summer.

o If you're in Nice for a week or more, a short-term apartment rental can be economical and give you more of a sense of living in the city.

Useful Website

Nice Pebbles (www. nicepebbles.com) offers dozens of rental apartments (one-/two-bedroom apartments from €80/100) and villas in and around Nice, all bookable through its website.

Best Budget

Hostel Meyerbeer Beach (☎ 04 93 88 95 65; www.hostelmeyerbeer. com; 15 rue Meyerbeer; dm €25-50, s €80-90, d

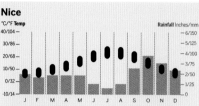

Nice
°C/°F Temp — Rainfall Inches/mm

When to Go

o **Winter** Family-friendly Christmas events in December and Carnaval celebrations in February.

o **Spring** Mild weather and markets filled with fresh produce and flowers. Beware region-wide hotel price hikes during Monaco's Grand Prix in May.

o **Summer** Perfect beach conditions; come in June or September to avoid the summer crush. Enjoy live music at the annual jazz festival in July.

o **Autumn** Golden light and lingering late-season beach days. Crowds dissipate as the weather cools.

€90-100; ☐ 7, 9, 22, 27, 59, 70 to Rivoli) The way every hostel should be: small, with welcoming staff and homey atmosphere.

Hôtel Villa St-Hubert (www.villasainthubert.com) Well-priced converted villa in a residential northern neighbourhood.

Hôtel Wilson (www. hotel-wilson-nice.com) Old-school budget hotel run by a local family.

Villa Saint-Exupéry Beach Hostel (www. villahostels.com) Large,

modern hostel with good facilities and friendly staff.

Hostel Les Camélias (www.hifrance.org) Traditional HI hostel in a grand old home with nice front garden.

Best Midrange

o **Hôtel Windsor** (www. hotelwindsornice.com) Boutique hotel with unique artwork gracing most rooms and the cafe-bar downstairs.

Nice Garden Hôtel (www.nicegardenhotel.com) Centrally located, well-kept boutique hotel.

Hôtel Villa Rivoli (www.villa-rivoli.com) Efficient, formal reception, fantastic location three blocks from the beach.

Hôtel Le Genève (www.hotel-le-geneve-nice.com) Unbeatable location in the heart of Nice's busiest nightlife district.

Hôtel Ozz (www.hotel-ozz.com) Quirky, colourful new hotel, part of the fun-loving Happyculture group.

Best Top End

Hôtel La Pérouse (www.hotel-la-perouse.com) Classy four-star perched on a steep hillside between Vieux Nice and the Mediterranean.

Hôtel Villa Victoria (www.villa-victoria.com) Palatial four-star with a delightful back patio.

Hôtel du Petit Palais (www.petitpalaisnice.com) Hillside villa in a residential neighbourhood with distant Mediterranean views.

Hôtel Villa Rose (www.hotelvillarose.com) Lovingly converted old villa north of the Libération market.

Exedra (http://nice.boscolohotels.com) Ultra-

luxurious five-star with its own private spa.

Arriving in Nice

Nice Côte d'Azur Airport

Located about 7km west of the city centre, France's second-largest airport offers direct flights with regular and low-cost airlines to cities throughout France and Europe, including London in only two hours. A few international flights also serve North Africa and the US. The airport has two terminals, linked by a free shuttle bus.

Excellent, low-cost public transport connects the airport to downtown, and its location near the A8 autoroute on Nice's western outskirts makes this a convenient place to pick up or drop off a rental car.

Bus Line 98 runs to Vieux Nice (€6, 30 minutes). Line 99 goes to Nice nVille train station (€6, 30 minutes).

Tram Line 2 (scheduled

for completion in 2019) runs to the city centre and the port (20 to 25 minutes).

Taxi Taxis from the airport to Nice's centre charge a flat rate of €32.

Nice Ville Train Station

Nice's main train station, at the north end of the city centre (1.5km inland from the waterfront), offers speedy rail connections to cities throughout France, including Paris in less than six hours. Train connections to neighbouring Italy are made through Ventimiglia, 55 minutes away on the French–Italian border.

Tram Line 1 (€1.50) runs south and east to Vieux Nice (10 minutes) and Garibaldi (15 minutes), or north to Libération (five minutes).

Port de Nice

Nice's ferry port is on the eastern edge of the city, just east across the hill from Vieux Nice. **Corsica Ferries** (☎04 92 00 42 76; www.corsicaferries.com; quai du Commerce; 🚌2 to Port

Lympia) and **Moby Lines** (☎08 00 90 11 44; www.mobylines.fr; Quai du Commerce; ☒2 to Port Lympia) offer regular service to Corsica (Bastia, Île Rousse, Ajaccio and Porto Vecchio) and Sardinia (Golfo Aranci).

Tram Line 2 (€1.50) runs west to place Garibaldi and destinations throughout the New Town.

Getting Around

Tram

Nice's excellent public transport system, operated by **Lignes d'Azur** (☎08 10 06 10 06; www.lignesdazur.com), includes a modern, dependable fleet of trams and buses.

The city's sleek trams (http://tramway.nice.fr) are great for getting across town, and are generally your best bet for journeys to the train station, the airport and the port.

The original line 1, opened in 2007,

charts a parabolic course through the city centre, connecting Nice Ville train station with Vieux Nice and Le Port-Garibaldi to the southeast and Libération to the north. Trams run from 4.25am to 1.35am, with service every four to five minutes between 7am and 8pm (less frequent at night and on Sundays). Nice's second tram line, scheduled for completion in 2019, runs east–west between the airport and the port, adding 20 new stations to the system.

Single-ride tickets cost €1.50 and can be purchased from machines at any tram stop. Frequent travellers can save money by purchasing one of the multiride tickets and passes sold at the same machines, valid on both trams and buses. All tickets (including day and week passes) must be validated at the beginning of each ride by inserting them into the machines provided on board the tram.

Bus

Buses, operated by Lignes d'Azur, are most convenient for destinations along the beachfront and in outlying neighbourhoods such as Cimiez.

Bus tickets cost €1.50 and include one connection, including intercity buses within the Alpes-Maritimes *département*. If you're using Nice's buses and trams a lot, consider purchasing a money-saving all-day ticket or mutliday pass. Buses are particularly handy for getting to the Musée Matisse and Musée Chagall in Cimiez.

Buses typically run every 10 to 15 minutes between 6am and 9pm. Between 9pm and 1am or 2am, night buses – numbered N1 through N5 and running every 30 to 60 minutes – fan out to various destinations around the city from their central terminus at Promenade des Arts.

Bus stops throughout the city have clear signs indicating which buses stop there. Tickets can be purchased at machines on the platform or on board the bus. All tickets (including day and week passes) must be validated at the beginning of each ride by inserting them into the machines provided on board.

Bicycle

Nice's bike-share program **Vélo Bleu** (📞 04 93 72 06 06; www.velobleu. org) offers a low-cost option for exploring the city. Pick up and return bikes at more than 100 stations around the city. One-day/weeklong subscriptions cost €1.50/5, plus usage: free for the first 30 minutes, €1 the next 30, then €2 per hour thereafter. Some stations are equipped with terminals to register directly with a credit card; otherwise you'll need a mobile phone.

The handy Vélo Bleu app allows you to find your nearest station, gives real-time information about the number of bikes available at each and calculates itineraries.

Walking

Since the weather is often good, and the city beautiful and pedestrian-friendly, walking is also an efficient and enjoyable way to get around, especially in Vieux Nice and Le Port-Garibaldi, and along the Promenade des Anglais.

Essential Information

Accessible Travel

Nice's public transport system has made great strides towards accessibility. Tram lines are equipped with wide doors and easy-access platforms for wheelchairs, and Mobil'azur (www. mobilazur.org) offers on-demand bus service for disabled visitors. Two of Nice's public beaches (Plage du Centenaire and Plage de Carras) are equipped for wheelchair use, with ramps down to the water, amphibious wheelchairs, and dedicated parking and restroom facilities.

Plage de Carras also offers facilities for visually impaired visitors: swimmers equipped with a special wrist strap can monitor their location using a system of four orientation beacons spaced 15m apart. Other services for the visually impaired include tactile strips at bus and tram stops to guide passengers to the boarding zone.

For further info see Nice Tourisme's handy *Nice Accessible: Guide Pratique* (www. nicetourisme.com/ nice-accessible), visit the French national website www.accessible.net, or download Lonely Planet's free Accessible Travel guide from http://lptravel.to/ AccessibleTravel.

Business Hours

Opening hours vary throughout the year. Our listings generally include high-season opening hours, plus hours for other seasons where these can be succinctly listed. Shoulder and low-season hours are typically shorter than high-season hours.

Banks 9am to noon and 2pm to 5pm Monday to Friday or Tuesday to Saturday

Bars 7pm to 1am

Cafes 7am to 11pm

Clubs 10pm to 3am, 4am or 5am Thursday to Saturday

Restaurants Noon to 2pm and 7pm to 10pm six days a week

Shops 10am to noon and 2pm to 7pm Monday to Saturday

Discount Cards

The French Riviera Pass (www.frenchrivierapass.com) includes access to a number of sights in Nice and along the Riviera. It is available online or at the Nice tourist office.

Included in the price of the pass (one/two/three days €26/38/56): in Nice, the Musée National Marc Chagall, Nice Le Grand Tour bus and guided walking tours; along the coast, the Musée Renoir in Cagnes, the Musée National Fernand Léger in Biot, the Jardin Exotique d'Èze, and the Jardin Exotique and Musée Océanographique in Monaco.

A Nice museum pass costs €10/20 per day/week and covers all city museums, except the Musée Chagall.

Electricity

Type C
230V/50Hz

Type E
230V/50Hz

LGBT+

Nice is a very LGBT-friendly city. The epicentre of its thriving gay community is in Le Port-Garibaldi.

AGLAE (www.facebook.com/AglaeLGBT) is Nice's main LGBT association, organising the city's Pink Parade pride festival each summer, along with other events throughout the year.

Nice's tourist office publishes an online guide (http://en.nicetourisme.com/nice-gay-friendly) to gay-friendly accommodation options and other businesses, including a list of bars and clubs.

Money
ATMs

The most cost-effective way to obtain local currency (euros) is via direct cash withdrawal from an ATM. Cash machines that accept international cards are readily available throughout Nice, including at the airport and train station.

Cash

You always get a better exchange rate in-country but it is a good idea to arrive in France with enough euro to take a taxi to a hotel if you have to.

Changing Money

o Commercial banks charge up to €5 per foreign-currency transaction – if they even bother to offer exchange services any more.

o *Bureaux de change* (exchange bureaus) are faster and easier, open longer hours and often give better rates than banks.

Credit Cards

o Credit and debit cards, accepted almost everywhere in France, are convenient, relatively secure and usually offer a reasonable exchange rate.

o Credit cards issued in France have embedded chips – you have to type in a PIN to make a purchase. Some businesses (most notably automated, unstaffed petrol stations) will only accept chip-and-PIN-enabled credit cards.

o Visa, MasterCard and Amex can be used in shops and supermarkets, and for train travel, car hire and motorway tolls.

o Don't assume that you can pay for a meal or a budget hotel with a credit card – enquire first.

o Getting cash with a credit card involves both fees (sometimes US$10 or more) and interest – ask your credit-card issuer for details. Debit-card fees are usually much less.

Tipping

Bars No tips for drinks served at bar; round to nearest euro for drinks served at the table.

Cafes & restaurants Prices automatically include a 15% service charge so there's no need to leave a tip; although many locals leave 5% to 10% extra if extremely satisfied with the service.

Hotel porters €1 to €2 per bag.

Taxis 10% to 15%.

Toilet attendants €0.50.

Tour guides €1 to €2 per person.

Public Holidays

The following *jours fériés* (public holidays) are observed in France:

New Year's Day (Jour de l'An) 1 January

Easter Sunday & Monday (Pâques & Lundi de Pâques) Late March/April

May Day (Fête du Travail) 1 May

Victoire 1945 8 May

Ascension Thursday (Ascension) May; on the 40th day after Easter

Pentecost/Whit Sunday & Whit Monday (Pentecôte & Lundi de Pentecôte) Mid-May to mid-June; on the seventh Sunday after Easter

Bastille Day/National Day (Fête Nationale) 14 July

Assumption Day (Assomption) 15 August

All Saints' Day (Toussaint) 1 November

Remembrance Day (L'onze Novembre) 11 November

Christmas (Noël) 25 December

The following are *not* public holidays in France: Shrove Tuesday (Mardi Gras; the first day of Lent); Maundy (or Holy) Thursday and Good

Dos & Donts

Conversation Use the formal *vous* when speaking to anyone unknown or older than you; the informal *tu* is reserved for close friends, family and children.

Churches Dress modestly (cover shoulders).

Drinks Asking for *une carafe d'eau* (free jug of tap water) in restaurants is acceptable. Never end a meal with a cappuccino or cup of tea. Play French and order *un café* (espresso).

French kissing Exchange *bisous* (cheek-skimming kisses) – at least two – with casual acquaintances and friends.

Friday, just before Easter; and Boxing Day (26 December).

Toilets

o Love them (as a sci-fi geek) or loathe them (as a claustrophobe), Nice's 24-hour self-cleaning toilets are here to stay. These mechanical WCs (you'll find 20 of them around the city) are free but allow limited time for dawdling: you have precisely 15 minutes before being (ooh-la-la!) exposed to passers-by. Green means *libre* (vacant) and red means *occupé* (occupied).

o There are also 11 pay toilets (adult/child €0.50/free), including

the centrally located ones along Promenade du Paillon.

o Some older establishments and motorway stops still have the hole-in-the-floor *toilettes à la turque* (squat toilets). Provided you hover, these are actually very hygienic, but take care not to get soaked by the flush.

o Keep some loose change handy for tipping toilet attendants, who keep a hawk-like eye on many of Nice's public toilets.

o The French are completely blasé about uni-sex toilets, so save your blushes when tiptoeing past the urinals to reach the ladies' loo.

Tourist Information

Nice's **main tourist office** (☏ 04 92 14 46 14; www.nicetourisme.com; 5 Promenade des Anglais; ⏰ 9am-7pm daily Jun-Sep, to 6pm Mon-Sat Oct-May; 📶; 🚌 8, 52, 62 to Massenet) provides a wealth of resources, including maps, brochures, information about attractions and help booking accommodation. There are branch offices at the **train station** (☏ 04 92 14 46 14; av Thiers; ⏰ 9am-7pm daily Jun-Sep, to 6pm Mon-Sat, 10am-5pm Sun Oct-May; 🚋 1 to Gare Thiers) and on **Promenade du Paillon** (Promenade du Paillon; ⏰ 10am-8pm Jun-Sep, to 5pm Dec; 🚋 1 to Masséna or Opéra-Vieille Ville).

Visas

Generally not required for stays of up to 90 days (or at all for EU nationals); some nationalities will require a Schengen visa.

For up-to-date information on visa requirements see www.diplomatie.gouv.fr.

o EU nationals and citizens of Iceland, Norway and Switzerland need only their passport or national identity card to enter France and work. However, nationals of the 12 countries that joined the EU in 2004 and 2007 are subject to residency and work limitations.

o Citizens of Australia, Canada, Hong Kong, Israel, Japan, Malaysia, New Zealand, Singapore, the USA and many Latin American countries do not need tourist visa for stays shorter than 90 days.

o Others must apply for a Schengen visa, allowing unlimited travel throughout 26 European countries for a 90-day period. Apply at the consulate of the country that's your first port of entry or will be your principal destination. Among other particulars, you must provide proof of travel and repatriation insurance, and prove you have sufficient money to support yourself.

o Tourist visas cannot be extended, except in emergencies (such as medical problems). Leave before your visa expires and reapply from outside France.

Language

The sounds used in spoken French can almost all be found in English. There are a couple of exceptions: nasal vowels (represented in our pronunciation guides by 'o' or 'u' followed by an almost inaudible nasal consonant sound 'm', 'n' or 'ng'), the 'funny' u sound ('ew' in our guides) and the deep-in-the-throat r. Bearing these few points in mind and reading our pronunciation guides below as if they were English, you'll be understood just fine. The markers (m) and (f) indicate the forms for male and female speakers.

To enhance your trip with a phrasebook, visit **lonelyplanet.com**. Lonely Planet iPhone phrasebooks are available in the Apple App store.

Basics

Hello.
Bonjour.　　　　　*bon·zhoor*

Goodbye.
Au revoir.　　　　*o·rer·vwa*

How are you?
Comment　　　　　*ko·mon*
allez-vous?　　　　*ta·lay·voo*

I'm fine, thanks.
Bien, merci.　　　*byun mair·see*

Please.
S'il vous plaît.　　*seel voo play*

Thank you.
Merci.　　　　　　*mair·see*

Excuse me.
Excusez-moi.　　*ek·skew·zay·mwa*

Sorry.
Pardon.　　　　　*par·don*

Yes./No.
Oui./Non.　　　　*wee/non*

I don't understand.
Je ne comprends　*zher ner kom·pron*
pas.　　　　　　　*pa*

Do you speak English?
Parlez-vous　　　*par·lay·voo*
anglais?　　　　　*ong·glay*

Eating & Drinking

..., please.
..., s'il vous plaît.　*... seel voo play*

A coffee	*un café*	*un ka·fay*
A table for two	*une table pour deux*	*ewn ta·bler poor der*
Two beers	*deux bières*	*der bee·yair*

I'm a vegetarian.
Je suis　　　　　*zher swee*
végétarien/　　　*vay·zhay·ta·ryun/*
végétarienne. (m/f)　*vay·zhay·ta·ryen*

That was delicious!
C'était délicieux!　*say·tay day·lee·syer*

The bill, please.
L'addition,　　　*la·dee·syon*
s'il vous plaît.　　*seel voo play*

Shopping

I'd like to buy ...
Je voudrais　　　*zher voo·dray*
acheter ...　　　　*ash·tay ...*

I'm just looking.
Je regarde.　　　*zher rer·gard*

How much is it?
C'est combien?　*say kom·byun*

It's too expensive.
C'est trop cher.　*say tro shair*

Can you lower the price?
Vous pouvez — voo poo-vay
baisser le prix? — bay-say ler pree

Emergencies

Help!
Au secours! — o skoor

Call the police!
Appelez la police! — a-play la po-lees

Call a doctor!
Appelez un — a-play un
médecin! — mayd-sun

I'm sick.
Je suis malade. — zher swee ma-lad

I'm lost.
Je suis perdu/ — zhe swee pair-dew
perdue. (m/f)

Where are the toilets?
Où sont les — oo son lay
toilettes? — twa-let

Time & Numbers

What time is it?
Quelle heure — kel er
est-il? — ay til

It's (eight) o'clock.
Il est (huit) — il ay (weet)
heures. — er

It's half past (10).
Il est (dix) heures — il ay (deez) er
et demie. — ay day-mee

morning	matin	ma-tun
afternoon	après-midi	a-pray-mee-dee
evening	soir	swar
yesterday	hier	yair
today	aujourd'hui	o-zhoor-dwee
tomorrow	demain	der-mun

Monday	lundi	lun-dee
Tuesday	mardi	mar-dee
Wednesday	mercredi	mair-krer-dee
Thursday	jeudi	zher-dee
Friday	vendredi	von-drer-dee
Saturday	samedi	sam-dee
Sunday	dimanche	dee-monsh

1	un	un
2	deux	der
3	trois	trwa
4	quatre	ka-trer
5	cinq	sungk
6	six	sees
7	sept	set
8	huit	weet
9	neuf	nerf
10	dix	dees
100	cent	son
1000	mille	meel

Transport & Directions

Where's ...?
Où est ...? — oo ay ...

What's the address?
Quelle est l'adresse? — kel ay la-dres

Can you show me (on the map)?
Pouvez-vous — poo-vay-voo
m'indiquer — mun-dee-kay
(sur la carte)? — (sewr la kart)

I want to go to ...
Je voudrais — zher voo-dray
aller à ... — a-lay a ...

Does it stop at (Amboise)?
Est-ce qu'il — es-kil
s'arrête à — sa-ret a
(Amboise)? — (om-bwaz)

I want to get off here.
Je veux — zher ver
descendre ici. — day-son-drer ee-see

Behind the Scenes

Send Us Your Feedback

We love to hear from travellers – your comments help make our books better. We read every word, and we guarantee that your feedback goes straight to the authors. Visit **lonelyplanet.com/contact** to submit your updates and suggestions.

Note: We may edit, reproduce and incorporate your comments in Lonely Planet products such as guidebooks, websites and digital products, so let us know if you don't want your comments reproduced or your name acknowledged. For a copy of our privacy policy visit lonelyplanet.com/privacy.

Gregor's Thanks

Merci beaucoup to the many French and Monégasque locals and expatriate residents who shared their insights about Nice and Monaco with me, especially Sarah Shepherd Barnes, Marion Pansiot, Clara Diaz Campuzano, Lucie Richard and Did Kwo. Back home, hugs to Gaen, Meigan and Chloe, who always make coming home the best part of the trip.

Acknowledgements

Cover photograph: Hôtel Negresco, Promenade des Anglais, Nice; Jon Arnold/AWL

This Book

This 1st edition of Lonely Planet's *Pocket Nice & Monaco* guidebook was researched, written and curated by Gregor Clark. This guidebook was produced by the following:

Destination Editor
Daniel Fahey

Senior Product Editor
Genna Patterson

Product Editor
Ronan Abayawickrema

Senior Cartographer
Mark Griffiths

Assisting Cartographer
Mick Garrett

Book Designer
Fergal Condon

Assisting Editors Janet Austin, Andrea Dobbin, Fionnuala Twomey

Cover Researcher
Naomi Parker

Thanks to Ben Buckner, Gwen Cotter, Evan Godt, Alicia Johnson, Claire Naylor, Karyn Noble, Matt Phillips, Martine Power, Gabrielle Stefanos, Angela Tinson

Index

See also separate subindexes for:

- 🍴 Eating p153
- 🍷 Drinking p153
- ✪ Entertainment p154
- 🔒 Shopping p154

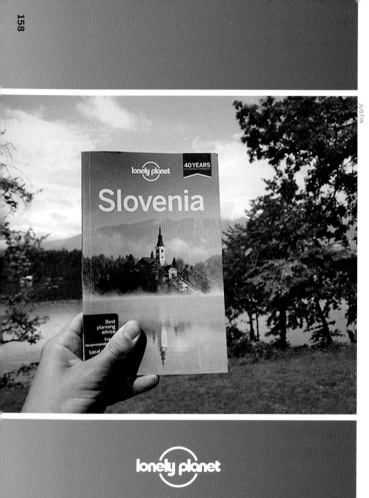

JUSTIN

LONELY PLANET IN THE **WILD**